MIGHTY
~ SPICE ~
EXPRESS
COOKBOOK

MIGHTY ~SPICE~ EXPRESS

COOKBOOK

FAST, FRESH AND FULL-ON FLAVORS
FROM STREET FOODS TO THE SPECTACULAR

JOHN GREGORY-SMITH

DUNCAN BAIRD PUBLISHERS

LONDON

DEDICATION

Sal and Al—I love you!

Mighty Spice Express Cookbook
John Gregory-Smith

Distributed in the USA and Canada by
Sterling Publishing Co., Inc.
387 Park Avenue South
New York, NY 10016-8810

First published in the UK and USA in 2013 by
Duncan Baird Publishers, an imprint of Watkins
Publishing Limited
Sixth Floor
75 Wells Street
London W1T 3QH

A member of Osprey Group

For information about custom editions, special sales,
premium and corporate purchases, please contact
Sterling Special Sales Department at 800-805-5489
or specialsales@sterlingpub.com.

Managing Editor: Grace Cheetham
Editor: Jan Cutler
Americanizer: Constance Novis
Art Direction and Design: Manisha Patel
Production: Uzma Taj
Commissioned Photography: William Lingwood
Food Stylist: Aya Nishimura
Prop Stylist: Wei Tang

ISBN: 978-1-84899-114-9

10 9 8 7 6 5 4 3 2 1

Typeset in Chaparral Pro and LD Bohemian Filigree
Color reproduction by PDQ, UK
Printed in China

Publisher's note While every care has been taken
in compiling the recipes for this book, Watkins
Publishing Limited, or any other persons who have
been involved in working on this publication, cannot
accept responsibility for any errors or omissions,
inadvertent or not, that may be found in the recipes
or text, nor for any problems that may arise as a
result of preparing one of these recipes. If you are
pregnant or breastfeeding or have any special dietary
requirements or medical conditions, it is advisable
to consult a medical professional before following
any of the recipes contained in this book. Ill or elderly
people, babies, young children and women who
are pregnant or breastfeeding should avoid recipes
containing raw meat or fish or uncooked eggs.

Notes on the recipes Unless otherwise stated:
• Use free-range eggs and poultry
• Use large eggs, and medium fruit and vegetables
• Use fresh ingredients, including herbs and chilies
• Wash all meat, fish and poultry, and all unpeeled
  vegetables and fruits (apart from mushrooms),
  as well as herbs and salads, and wipe mushrooms
  before preparation
• 1 tsp. = 5ml   1 tbsp. = 15ml   1 cup = 240ml

CONTENTS

INTRODUCTION

Food, recipes, cooking, spices and eating are my life, so when my publisher asked me to follow up my first book, *Mighty Spice Cookbook*, I was thrilled. I had already been working on new recipes, so it was a great time to pop the question.

The *Mighty Spice Cookbook* set out to show everyone how simple it was to cook with spices. I never used more than five spices in each recipe and I kept the ingredients supermarket friendly. It made sense that the next step would be to show everyone how fast it is to cook with spices, whatever the occasion. *Mighty Spice Express* was born, and we started putting ideas down. I always like to introduce new recipes and flavors, so I travel abroad for my research. I carefully chose the countries to visit that would give me the most inspiration for express cooking.

"Express" obviously meant street food, and this has been a real inspiration for the book. Street food shows the best a place has to offer and a snapshot of what's hot right now. It is always served fast and furious, and can be hot or cold, savory or sweet. But, guaranteed, it will be tasty, fresh and cooked to perfection. Quite simply, if the food doesn't cut the mustard it won't be there the following morning.

DUCKING AND DIVING IN FEZ

Mighty Spice Express took me to the stunning city of Fez in Morocco, which has the oldest working *medina*—or old part of the city—in the world. This means a vast expanse of car-free city where people live and trade. The buildings are packed so tightly together that most of the streets are actually narrow passages supported by huge wooden struts, which are best navigated by frequent ducking—Bilbo Baggins and co. would have been perfectly at home.

To an outsider, the city is a maze, and one that needs a guide. Luckily, I had the best in Gail Leonard. Gail organized street-food tours of fabulous Fez and we met one cold January morning by the magnificent Blue Gate. After coffee, we stopped for a sassy sweetbread sandwich—fried sweetbreads that were served in a bun with spices and finely chopped onions. It was delicious and, strangely, it worked as a great pick-me-up first thing in the morning.

It was also to serve as the inspiration for my Blue Gate Fez Sandwich in the Mighty Bites chapter.

The natural slope of the ancient city took us south. We wound through narrow passages lit by hazy shafts of light and emerged onto one of the main market streets in Fez. Chickens clucked while waiting for someone's pot. Alongside the chickens were camel heads, spices, herbs, beautiful juicy strawberries, olives, nuts, harissa paste and a wonderful little stand that sold *bessara*. *Bessara* is a breakfast soup made from fava beans. It's rich and thick and perfect for keeping hungry workers full until lunchtime. My bowl was seasoned heavily with chili and cumin and tasted utterly sublime.

SPECIALTIES FROM THE SEA AT ESSAOUIRA

After Fez I took the train south to the remarkable coastal town of Essaouira. There are times when my job is unbelievable, and this was one of them. I arrived at this magical place and went for a long run along the beach. Kite surfers took off in the sparkling waters around me, horses galloped along the shore and the whole time the setting sun framed the walled city like a movie. I even made some new friends of the canine variety, who followed me all the way back to my hotel. This became slightly awkward when I had to navigate through the fashionable cafés of the town, red-faced, sweating and trailed by stray dogs.

Mighty Spice Express is about making any meal an occasion fast. Fish and shellfish cook quickly, and Essaouira fed my mind, tummy and soul with seafood. I was inspired at every turn, especially when I had dinner at Sam's—not quite the evocative Moroccan-nights' name I would have come up with for the best seafood place in town, but who am I to judge? Sam's was located at the end of the pier, past the rocking fishing boats, dried nets and slightly spooky seagulls. From the outside the restaurant looked like a blue-and-yellow lobster shack from *Family Guy*. Inside, the decor of jewel-encrusted spider crabs and black-and-white photographs of Hollywood stars was equally baffling, but the food was on the money. It was coastal Moroccan with a classic French twist—wow! Get in a taxi right now, ask for Sam's and order the monkfish skewers. You will not be disappointed.

COCONUT, FENUGREEK AND THE BRIGHT COLORS OF INDIA

The next stop for my research was India—Goa to be exact—where the coconut curries and fresh coastal food were all made in no time. Every town has its local food heroes, and in Dabolim it's Rita Shinde. From her beautiful garden, Rita taught the local women how to make the excellent, fresh food of southern India. Now, not being local or a woman, I was very lucky she took me on. We went through all the classic Goan dishes, then she taught me about the tamarind-based Hindi food and, finally, the Catholic Goan cuisine, which used the pungent local vinegar in abundance. Her *reshado* sauce has been an utter revelation for me and I am happy to say that it has inspired several of the dishes in this book.

After Goa, I traveled north to Mumbai—a melting pot of all that India has to offer. This particular trip was made extra special by two people, Lizzie and Amish. With Lizzie's military organizational skills and Amish's local knowledge, I ate everything in Mumbai! They even arranged a low-key visit to Dharavi, one of the famed city slums. I don't know why, but for some reason I had been geared up for a massive bout of Western guilt. I expected to see horrific things, but the trip was one of the most amazing experiences I have ever had in my whole life.

The slum—wrongly named because it suggests something bleak—is a fully functioning city within a city. Hundreds of thousands of people live, work and socialize here. Working conditions are pretty terrible, but there is such life and energy! Everyone was busy working in industry—sorting plastics, building machinery, sewing clothes, making soap and producing most of Mumbai's poppadoms. There was more of a sense of community in that place than I have ever felt anywhere else before. Everyone knew one another. They chatted, they worked and they went to the main street to eat, drink, shop and even go to the movies. The residential areas were spotless. People took pride in where they lived. For every bit of dreary gray, the inhabitants' love of bright colors prevailed. For every funny odor, the wonderful smells of fenugreek and coconut oil filled the air. Even the constant noise of the traffic was drowned out by high-pitched Hindi love songs. I loved it and even now I can feel goose bumps while I'm writing about my time there. I feel honored to have been to Dharavi.

EATING FOR FOUR IN THE FAR EAST

The final area my research for *Mighty Spice Express* took me to the Far East. Having already spent time in Thailand and Laos, I decided to expand my knowledge and go to Seoul and northeastern China to learn something new. Seoul was crazy—a vast metropolis of cool people, wicked food and technology that would have humbled the Starship Enterprise.

I kicked off my first night by exploring the low-level restaurants that lined the cross streets between the skyscrapers of Gangnam District. For some reason, every restaurant I went into threw me out. Tired and hungry, and feeling a bit like I hadn't been picked for the sports team, I retired to my hotel. Thankfully, the next day I was informed that it was not because I was weird and Western, but because the restaurants in question served huge sharing dishes that were way too big for one person. Armed with this invaluable local information I returned, asked for a table for four and ate everything myself.

The next morning, my guide took me around the north of the city. First I learned how to make precious kimchi, which is the cornerstone of every Korean meal. Next, we went on a serious street-food tour. We ate so well: *pa jun*, a fantastic Korean pancake; giant steamed dumplings filled with pork and scallions; *bibimbap*, a classic rice dish; grilled kebabs; noodle soup with clams; and spicy fried tofu. The choices seemed endless—and everything was delicious.

AIRBORNE EXERCISES AND SPECTACULAR BARBECUES

There are not enough superlatives in the world for me to describe China. Shanghai, for example, is the only place where you can order scorpion, dim sum, sea cucumber and foie gras all at once. Several years ago my great friends, Mike and Annie, introduced me to the food of Dongbai, an area of northeastern China where Annie was born. Since then, I have been obsessed with going to this part of the world, and luckily it fitted the bill for *Mighty Spice Express*. I found myself on a flight with Mike and Annie heading to the city of Shenyang to learn about Dongbai food and their famous barbecue. All that I love about China happened on that flight. At one point, the stoic passengers, who had sat so silently, were drawn to attention by the cabin crew who had formed a line down the middle of the plane. They proceeded to demonstrate a series of exercises intended to help combat cramp and deep vein thrombosis that wouldn't have looked out of place at a Spice Girls concert. The silence broke and everyone joined in expressively copying the moves. The routine culminated in hands that were crossed over shoulders, then flying into the air for an ecstatic double clap, and then the passengers returned to the demure silence of before. It was amazing and so random, just like the rest of the country.

We went straight from the airport to a restaurant called Little South Island BBQ that was owned by a friend of Annie's. It was here that I learned the secret of Dongbai food, their barbecue and the true meaning of Chinese hospitality. Lots of things in China happen behind closed doors, including "cutting loose," which is exactly what happened at lunch. While the rest of the restaurant was filled with hushed diners, we were holed up in a private room surrounded by friends, family, food and way too much alcohol. Every sublime dish was lovingly explained to me by my hosts and followed by a lethal dose of *baiju*, a gigantically boozy Chinese liquor. We must have eaten about 40 different dishes. You can do the math for the shots! Both the food and barbecue were an eye opener, and I learned techniques and seasonings that I had never seen before—boy, are you in for a treat!

ABOUT THIS BOOK

Mighty Spice Express is all about making fantastic food in no time. To achieve this, I have developed recipes using techniques, spices, cuts of meat and fish, cooking methods and ingredients that all work toward making delicious express meals and snacks for any occasion.

Spices are at the heart of the recipes in this book. The more I travel the more I learn new ways to use these fabulous ingredients. They are truly versatile and it's fascinating how the same spices, used in a different way, can take the food on your table from one country to another. For me, spices offer an escape and transport me somewhere else while I eat. They add the flavors, color, heat and fragrance of some of the most beautiful and exotic places in the world. With a pinch of cumin, some grated ginger or a few slices of lemongrass I can whip up something wonderful and transform my apartment in East London into the best exotic restaurant in the world.

As you look through the book, you'll notice that each recipe includes pictures of the spices used, so you'll be able to see at a glance which ones you will need to make it.

This book is packed full of exciting recipes, which all work in the times I have given. I have lovingly time-tested each one, over and over again, to make sure that they all work perfectly. The key was getting the preparation and cooking done at exactly the right time. So that you can achieve the same fast results, I have included all the preparation in the recipe method rather than in the ingredients list. While part of the dish is cooking you'll be preparing the ingredients for the next stage. The recipes are not complicated, and the way I have designed them means you'll be making the most of your time in the kitchen. As long as you don't go off piste you'll nail the recipes easily.

I hope you'll enjoy making and eating this collection of recipes as much as I do and that this book will help to make cooking any meal an express experience for you.

EXPRESS FLAVOR ESSENTIALS

Stuff your cupboard and stock up your fridge with some basics and you'll be able to rustle up a spicy meal at any time.

A LITTLE SOUTHEASTERN ASIA

Coconut Creamed coconut is fresh coconut formed into a solid block. The high fat content means it will melt into a sauce to thicken and enrich it. It can also be grated over salads or onto broiled meats where it will melt through the food. Coconut cream and coconut milk are made by squeezing water through the ground flesh of a fresh coconut. The milky liquid from the first press is coconut cream. It has the highest fat content, making it rich and flavorsome. The remaining pulp is mixed with more water for a second pressing, giving the slightly milder-tasting coconut milk.

Fish sauce This highly smelly sauce is salty and pungent. It can be used instead of salt and to add flavor to curries, soups, stir-fries and salads.

Hoisin sauce is a Chinese condiment that can be used in stir-fries and as a dip for roasted meats, fish and vegetables. It has a rich soy–salty taste and it doesn't need cooking.

Oyster sauce is a slightly sweet condiment that is used all over southeastern Asia. The thick brown sauce is made from soybeans and oyster extract, tasting both sweet and savory. Look for the highest percentage of oyster extract when purchasing.

Rice wine vinegar This provides the classic southeastern Asian sour flavor. It's great for dipping sauces and salad dressings. The taste is very tart, so it always needs to be balanced by something sweet or hot.

Soy sauce The brilliant *umami* taste (meaning "pleasant savory taste" in Japanese) that soy sauce gives to food is superb. Use it in stews instead of salt to create depth of flavor. I have used light and dark soy sauces here. Traditionally, light is used as a seasoning and dark to add color. I find the light salty and fresh, and the dark much richer with a more complex flavor.

Sweet chili sauce is the ultimate ready-made dipping sauce. It works especially well in a salad dressing with a good squeeze of lime to balance out the sweetness. It gives instant flavor with zero effort.

FAVE SAVORIES

Pitted olives Olives have a good savory taste that complements many dishes. Scatter them all over salads and tagines, or use them in a salsa or pesto where their intense saltiness works really well.

Preserved lemons possess a superb and unique flavor, and are now easy to buy. Just cut them into quarters, remove and discard the flesh and finely chop or slice the rind. They work in tagines, stews, soups, salads, rice dishes and kebabs, and provide an instant Moroccan flavor.

Sun-dried tomatoes and paste For this book I have used sun-dried tomatoes (in oil) in salsas and sauces for their intense smoky and salty flavor. The paste adds the same big flavor without chopping or blending.

Tahini Made with sesame seeds, tahini is a classic Middle Eastern ingredient. The flavor is rich and intense, and a little goes a long way. It works well as a dip mixed with yogurt and is one of the main ingredients in hummus. It lasts for ages, so you'll get lots of use from one jar.

Tomato passata and paste So many recipes are tomato-based, and if you are short of time, tomato passata (sieved tomatoes) and paste can be a quick solution for adding flavor. They are already cooked, so the tomato richness is intensified, and they just need to be reheated.

Worcestershire sauce This quintessentially British ingredient is bound to be lying around in one of your kitchen cupboards. It's made from vinegar, anchovies and spices, so it's not that far removed from the fishy south-eastern Asian condiments. It adds an unusual flavor, which melts into the background when used in curries, spice pastes and salad dressings.

VERSATILE SPICES

Chili powder and chili flakes Sometimes there's no time for chopping, so keep chili powder and chili flakes on hand for an instant spicy kick.

Chinese five-spice powder is a mixture of spices, including star anise, fennel, cinnamon, cloves, Szechuan pepper, ginger and nutmeg, and there are endless combinations. It has a strong aniseed flavor that works well with soy sauce, making it perfect to add to Chinese dishes.

Chipotle chilies These are wood-smoked jalapeños, which add an incredibly woody, smoky flavor to everything, including salsas, stews, spice rubs and marinades. The taste is authentically Mexican. The chilies are dried and need a little soaking in warm water or a hot sauce to soften. They also blend into a powder easily, which is perfect for salsas, rubs or marinades.

Chocolate, made from cacao, is a very old spice that was used by the Mayans of Central America. The cacao beans are roasted and mixed with cocoa butter and sugar. It has a rich, spicy and nutty flavor, which develops on your palate as it melts. Use it in sweet and savory dishes. Use semisweet or bittersweet chocolate with the highest cocoa content for cooking.

Cinnamon is a classic spice that is used the world over. It loves everything from lamb and rice to chocolate and ice cream. I use cinnamon in ground or stick form in my recipes. If you don't have cinnamon sticks in the cupboard, you can also substitute ½ teaspoon ground cinnamon for a 2-inch stick.

Cumin and coriander These are the two ingredients that I would recommend to anyone who is starting to use spices. They have a wonderful flavor, they work beautifully together and can be used in many types of cuisines. Keep both ground cumin and the seeds on hand, so that you can use the seeds as a base in hot oil to flavor a dish and add some texture.

Smoked paprika The flavor-to-effort ratio of this superb spice is off the scale, which makes it my kitchen-cupboard essential. This bright red powder is made from ground wood-smoked peppers and/or chilies, which have a massive smoky taste. You can add it to any savory dish to inject some flavor, as well as using it in salsas, marinades, rubs and salad dressings.

THE RIGHT OIL AND VINEGAR FOR THE JOB

Olive oil and extra virgin olive oil have a much stronger flavor than other oils. This is great for cooking Mediterranean-style dishes and making salad dressings. Use the olive oil for cooking and the extra virgin olive oil for dressings (it loses flavor once heated). All olive oils have a low smoke point and so are not suitable for cooking with fierce heat, such as stir-frying.

Peanut oil is the best oil for making stir-fries, because it has a high smoke point, which is important when frying over high heat. It also has a mild flavor so it won't interfere with the other flavors in the dish.

Sesame oil has a rich, roasted-sesame flavor, which is perfect in salad dressings, rubs and marinades. Excellent, too, added at the end of a stir-fry.

Sunflower oil has a high smoke point. It's very mild in flavor and cheap to buy. I use it for shallow- and deep-frying in this book.

Balsamic vinegar This classic Italian sweet vinegar is great for roasts, stir-fries and salad dressings.

Cider vinegar is a versatile vinegar. It is not too tart and it works well as a substitute if you can't find rice wine vinegar.

Red wine vinegar has a lovely flavor that is not as sharp as the other vinegars and is perfect to use in cooking and as a base for salad dressings.

FRESH FLAVORINGS

Garlic is a staple ingredient in every kitchen I have visited all over the world. It adds a sweet, mellow background flavor when cooked slowly, or a stronger fiery flavor when cooked quickly.

Ginger has a fresh peppery taste that is wonderful in curries, stir-fries and salad dressings. Fresh gingerroot will last in the fridge for up to a week.

Green and red chilies Fresh chilies last up to 10 days in the fridge and add heat and vibrancy to dishes both savory and sweet. I love to have multiple chili options at home for my cooking.

Lemongrass can make a curry taste fragrant and authentic, and the delicate citrus flavor will transform a stir-fry. It goes well with soy sauce, particularly in marinades. Stored in the fridge it will last for several weeks.

Lemons and limes All recipes need balance, and "sour" is a key flavor in southeastern Asian cooking. Lemons and limes freshen everything up and ignite other flavors to make them stronger.

Parsley and cilantro These two awesome herbs add color and freshness to everything. I can't live without them. Store them in the fridge.

MIGHTY BITES

Here is a collection of my favorite snacks, and they are bursting with different flavors from around the world. Loads of the recipes were inspired by street food, which is quite simply the best fast food there is. Many are great for parties, when you want something to munch on while standing and having a chat with your friends, holding a drink in your other hand. With recipes ranging from Los Danzantes Empanadas, made with shrimp and mozzarella, to spicy Thai Pork Sliders, all the recipes serve 2 and there is something here for everyone. My Fried Chili Corn, sprinkled with sea salt, is quite literally "TV sports and cold beers" best buddy, but the greatest part about Mighty Bites is that all the recipes can be thrown together in 15 minutes or less.

Chicken Tenders with Sweet Chili & Basil Sauce SERVES **2**   READY IN **10 MINUTES**

I am a sucker for chicken with a dip, which is probably a hangover from my dad's obsession with chicken and mayonnaise. My cheeky chicken snack uses little chicken tenders, which cook in no time. It's served with a punchy dipping sauce that is made with sweet chili sauce, fresh green basil and wonderful fennel seeds, which liven it up with a background hint of aniseed.

4 mini chicken tenders (about
   7 ounces total weight)
2½ tablespoons olive oil
1 handful of basil leaves
1 teaspoon fennel seeds

3 tablespoons sweet chili sauce
½ lime
sea salt and freshly ground black
   pepper

HEAT A GRILL PAN over high heat until smoking. Meanwhile, brush the chicken with ½ tablespoon of the oil. Place it on the pan and reduce the heat to medium. Grill the chicken 3 to 4 minutes on each side, or until golden and cooked through.

WHILE THE CHICKEN COOKS, put the basil, the remaining oil and a good pinch of salt and pepper into a mini food processor or blender, and blend until smooth. Pour the oil mixture into a serving bowl. Gently crush the fennel seeds with the flat side of a knife blade or using a mortar and pestle, and add them to the serving bowl. Add the sweet chili sauce, then squeeze in the juice of the lime and mix well. Serve the golden chicken with the sweet chili and basil sauce.

Blue Gate Fez Sandwich SERVES **2** READY IN **15 MINUTES**

This awesome sandwich was inspired by a street-food vendor who was parked beside the magnificent Blue Gate in Fez, Morocco. It was a freezing-cold morning, and this wicked sandwich, packed with crunchy onions, spices and fresh herbs, was the perfect way to warm up. My version uses chicken instead of offal (sorry Fez) but it shares the big flavors.

2 skinless chicken breasts
1 tablespoon olive oil
½ red onion
½ lemon
8 pitted green olives
1 handful of parsley leaves
2 wholewheat buns

2 tablespoons sun-dried
   tomato paste
3 tablespoons mayonnaise
½ teaspoon ground cumin
a pinch of chili powder
sea salt and freshly ground
   black pepper

LAY THE CHICKEN BREASTS on a cutting board and, using a rolling pin, bash them out until they are ½ inch thick. Season one side with a good pinch of salt and pepper. Heat the oil in a large skillet over medium heat and fry the chicken, seasoned-side down first, 3 to 3½ minutes on each side, or until golden and cooked through.

WHILE THE CHICKEN COOKS, peel and slice the onion into thin strips, then add to a mixing bowl. Squeeze the juice of the lemon all over the onions and mix well. Finely chop the olives and parsley and set aside.

CUT THE BUNS IN HALF and spread the sun-dried tomato paste over one half of each, and the mayonnaise over the other half. Now add the cooked chicken and season with the cumin and chili powder. Scatter the chicken with the onions, olives and parsley, and set the other half of each bun on top. Serve immediately while hot.

Thai Pork Sliders SERVES 2 READY IN 10 MINUTES

These lovely little sliders (small hamburgers) are so tasty and quick to make. Using really good-quality pork sausages means that the meat is already the perfect consistency to incorporate all the fragrant Thai seasonings. A fresh lime hit at the end accentuates the flavors, and the sweet chili sauce is the perfect dunking partner.

½-inch piece fresh gingerroot
1 garlic clove
1 lemongrass stalk
½ red chili
¼ teaspoon freshly ground black pepper

1 small handful of basil leaves
1 teaspoon fish sauce
7 ounces best-quality pork sausages
1 tablespoon olive oil

TO SERVE
1 lime
sweet chili sauce

PEEL THE GINGER and garlic, then remove the tough outer leaves from the lemongrass and cut off the ends of the stalks. Put the ginger and garlic into a mini food processor, and add the lemongrass, chili, black pepper, basil and fish sauce. Blend to a smooth paste. Scoop the paste into a mixing bowl and set aside.

CUT OPEN THE SAUSAGES, peel off the skins and add the meat to the mixing bowl with the spice paste. Combine together well and divide the pork into 6 portions. Flatten each portion into the shape of a mini burger patty—*voilà* sliders!

PLACE THE OIL in a large skillet over medium heat and fry the sliders 1½ to 2 minutes on each side, or until golden and crispy.

WHILE THE PORK COOKS, cut the lime in half and pour the sweet chili sauce into a serving bowl. Serve the sliders with the lime halves and sweet chili sauce.

Hummus Beiruti SERVES **2** READY IN **10 MINUTES**

To me, hummus rocks! My Hummus Beiruti is a slightly dressed-up version of the awesome dip. I make a deliciously light hummus, then top it with lovely sweet lamb that has been fried, super-fast, with allspice, cumin and cinnamon. The hit of spiced lamb melts through the hummus and makes it even more unbelievably tasty. This is ready in less than 10 minutes, so there's always time for a bit of happy hummus eating.

¼ cup olive oil
4 ounces ground lamb
¼ teaspoon ground allspice
¼ teaspoon ground cumin

a pinch of ground cinnamon
1½ lemons
2 pieces of pita bread
14-ounce can chickpeas

1 garlic clove
2 tablespoons tahini
sea salt

HEAT 1 TABLESPOON OF THE OIL in a skillet over high heat and add the lamb. Stir-fry 2 minutes, then reduce the heat to medium. Add the allspice, cumin and cinnamon, and squeeze in the juice of ½ lemon. Cook 2 to 3 minutes, stirring occasionally, until the lamb is cooked through.

WHILE THE LAMB COOKS, put the pita bread into a toaster and toast until crunchy. Add the chickpeas to a colander and give them a good rinse. Drain off any excess water and put them into a blender or food processor with the remaining olive oil. Peel the garlic and add it to the blender with the tahini and a scant ¼ cup water. Season with salt. Squeeze in the juice of the remaining lemon and blend until smooth. Serve the hummus with the lamb on top, and toasted pita on the side.

Korean Kebabs SERVES 2 READY IN 10 MINUTES

As I roamed the high-tech streets of Seoul in Korea, I found little food stands nestled in the side streets offering the tastiest snacks. My favorites were these beef kebabs, which were barbecued over hot coals and served with sticky marinade and scattered with crunchy sesame seeds. What is great about them is that they are so quick and easy to make yet they taste out of this world.

6-ounce sirloin steak
1 garlic clove
1¼ tablespoons soy sauce

2 teaspoons honey
½ teaspoon freshly ground black
   pepper

1 teaspoon sesame oil
½ teaspoon peanut oil
1 teaspoon sesame seeds

CUT THE STEAK into long, thin strips, about 1⁄16 inch thick, and add them to a mixing bowl.

HEAT A GRILL PAN over high heat until smoking. Meanwhile, peel and crush the garlic. Add it to the bowl with the steak, followed by the soy sauce, honey, black pepper, sesame oil and peanut oil. Mix well to coat, then thread the strips of steak onto six metal skewers.

GRILL THE KEBABS 1 to 1½ minutes on each side, or until charred on the outside but still pink and juicy in the center. Transfer the kebabs to a serving dish, scatter with the sesame seeds and serve.

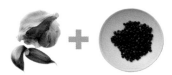

Moroccan Paper Bag Sardines SERVES **2**   READY IN **15 MINUTES**

I first ate this fabulous snack in Fez. After a hard day's eating, I stopped at a tiny hole-in-the-wall where I was served crisp sardines in a paper bag with a wedge of lemon. What I loved was the texture of the batter. It was an even mixture of flour and semolina, which gave even more crunch to the fish. The subtle spicing, which was mixed into the batter, really brought it to life. Just a little cumin and chili powder, and you're good to go.

sunflower oil, for shallow-frying
heaped ⅓ cup all-purpose flour
heaped ⅓ cup semolina
2 teaspoons ground cumin
1 teaspoon chili powder
8 small sardines, cleaned

scant ⅔ cup yogurt
1 teaspoon harissa or chili paste
1 lemon
sea salt

POUR THE OIL into a large frying pan to a depth of ½ inch and place over medium-high heat. Meanwhile, sift the flour into a large mixing bowl and add the semolina, cumin and chili powder, then season with salt. Pour in a scant ⅔ cup cold water and beat to a thick batter. Add the sardines and gently mix to coat completely in batter.

SHAKE ANY EXCESS BATTER off the sardines and shallow-fry them in the hot oil 3 to 4 minutes on each side, or until beautifully golden and cooked through. Carefully remove the sardines from the oil using a slotted spoon and place them on a dish lined with paper towels to drain.

WHILE THE SARDINES DRAIN, add the yogurt to a serving bowl and stir in the harissa. Lightly season with salt and mix well. Cut the lemon into wedges. Serve the sardines with the harissa yogurt and lemon wedges on the side.

Crab & Scallion Pancakes SERVES 2   READY IN 15 MINUTES

This is a classic Korean snack and one that I know you'll love. It's actually called *pa-jun* and is an egg-based pancake flavored with soy and chili, then stuffed with beautifully sweet crabmeat, fresh herbs and oyster sauce. Typically, it would be served with a spicy kimchi. If you can get hold of some, give it a try. But it really is just so good on its own.

⅓ cup all-purpose flour
1 egg
¼ teaspoon crushed chili flakes
1 teaspoon light soy sauce
3 scallions
1 handful of cilantro leaves

scant ⅔ cup cooked white crabmeat
½-inch piece fresh gingerroot
1 tablespoon peanut oil
2 tablespoons oyster sauce

ADD THE FLOUR to a large mixing bowl, pour in ¼ cup water and crack in the egg. Season with the chili flakes and soy sauce, and beat everything together to form a smooth batter.

TRIM THE SCALLIONS, then finely chop the scallions and cilantro leaves, and add half to the batter. Mix well. Put the other half into a separate mixing bowl and add the crab. Peel the ginger, then grate it onto the crab and mix it in well.

HEAT HALF THE OIL in a large skillet over medium heat and pour in half the egg batter. Cook 1 minute on each side, then transfer to a serving plate. Keep the pancake warm while you cook a second pancake in the same way.

BRUSH THE TOP OF EACH PANCAKE with one-quarter of the oyster sauce. Divide the crab mixture into 2 portions and arrange 1 portion in a line down the center of each pancake. Fold the pancakes in half and transfer them to serving plates. Drizzle each portion with the remaining oyster sauce to serve.

Jonny's Dumplings   SERVES **2**   READY IN **15 MINUTES**

Dim sum is somewhat of an obsession of mine. From the super-slimy rice rolls to the dry, delicate, steamed parcels of a high-brow Hong Kong hotel, I can't get enough of them. The ritual of ticking the little boxes on the menu, waiting for the steamer trolley and then dipping the glory into various soy, chili and vinegar condiments is a complete pleasure to me. To make, though, it's not such fun. However, I really wanted to get something into this book, and after eating cabbage-leaf dim sum at a restaurant called Jonny's in Korea, I thought, "bring it on," and I came up with this quick version.

2 large green savoy cabbage leaves
¼ red chili
1 scallion
1 small handful of cilantro leaves

5½ ounces raw shelled jumbo shrimp
¼ teaspoon Chinese five-spice powder

1 teaspoon light soy sauce, plus extra to serve
1 tablespoon peanut oil

PUT THE CABBAGE LEAVES in a heatproof bowl, cover with boiling water and let soften 2 to 3 minutes. Meanwhile, seed the chili and trim the scallion. Place them both in a blender or food processor and add the cilantro leaves, shrimp, Chinese five-spice powder and soy sauce. Blend until smooth.

DRAIN THE CABBAGE LEAVES in a colander and refresh under cold water a few seconds until they are cool enough to handle. Gently squeeze out any excess water and place them on a cutting board. Cut out the stems and cut the leaves into 2 halves. Put one-quarter of the shrimp mixture onto each piece of cabbage leaf and roll them up, tucking in the sides. They should look like roundish egg rolls.

HEAT THE OIL in a skillet over high heat and add the dumplings, fold-side down. Cook 2 minutes, then pour boiling water into the side of the skillet to a depth of ¹⁄₁₆ inch. Cover, reduce the heat to medium and steam 4 minutes. Remove the lid and cook 2 to 3 minutes, or until most of the water has evaporated and the dumplings are cooked through. Serve with light soy sauce on the side for dipping.

Los Danzantes Empanadas SERVES **2** READY IN **10 MINUTES**

Traditionally, *empanadas* are deep-fried Mexican snacks that look like little Cornish pasties. They are crunchy and delicious, but quite time-consuming to make. These *empanadas* are an express version. I use a soft flour tortilla for the shell, stuff it with shrimp, mozzarella, smoky sun-dried tomatoes, chili, scallions and cilantro leaves, then pan-fry it to get a crisp outside and an oozing filling. They take only 10 minutes to make, so I am sure you'll forgive me for not being an *empanada* purist.

2 scallions
¼ red chili
heaped ⅓ cup drained sun-dried
   tomatoes in oil
1 small handful of cilantro leaves

1 flour tortilla
1 tablespoon olive oil
2¼ ounces mozzarella cheese
3½ ounces cooked shelled shrimp
¼ lime

TRIM THE SCALLIONS, then place them into a mini food processor. Add the chili, sun-dried tomatoes and cilantro, and blend to a rough paste. Place the tortilla on a cutting board and spread with the paste, leaving a ½-inch gap around the edge.

HEAT THE OIL in a nonstick skillet over high heat. Meanwhile, tear the mozzarella into bite-size pieces and scatter it, with the shrimp, all over one half of the tortilla. Wet your finger with cold water and then rub it around the border of the tortilla. Fold the tortilla in half and press the edges together to seal.

CAREFULLY PUT THE EMPANADA in the hot pan, reduce the heat to medium and cook 1½ to 2 minutes on each side, or until warmed through and golden. Cut the empanada in half and transfer to serving plates. Cut the lime quarter in half and serve with each empanada.

Dosa Rosti SERVES 2 READY IN 15 MINUTES

My *dosa rosti* is a super-quick southern Indian-inspired snack. The grated potato and onion cook down fast and take on all the flavor of the spices. I love the added layer of heat from the hot lime pickle slathered over the roti. This is fast food, Indian style.

1 large potato (about 7 ounces in weight)
½ red onion
1 teaspoon ground cumin
1 teaspoon ground coriander

¼ teaspoon chili powder
¼ teaspoon turmeric
2 tablespoons peanut oil
1 teaspoon mustard seeds
1 tomato

1 handful of cilantro leaves
2 plain roti
1 tablespoon hot lime pickle
½ lime
sea salt

PEEL THE POTATO and onion, then grate both into a mixing bowl. Add the cumin, coriander, chili powder and turmeric, and season with salt, then mix everything together well.

HEAT THE OIL in a large skillet over high heat and add the mustard seeds. Allow them to crackle a couple of seconds, then add the potatoes and onion, and stir-fry 3 minutes. Add a scant ½ cup water, stir well, then cover and reduce the heat to medium. Cook 4 to 5 minutes, stirring occasionally, until soft.

WHILE THE POTATO COOKS, cut the tomato in half, squeeze out the seeds, finely chop the flesh and set aside. Finely chop the cilantro leaves and reserve.

PUT THE ROTI onto a cutting board and spread each one evenly with the lime pickle. To serve the dish, squeeze the juice of the lime into the cooked potatoes and stir well. Divide the potato mixture between each roti, scatter with the chopped tomato and cilantro leaves, and serve.

MUMBAI MAGIC, HOLY COWS & PANEER

The city of Mumbai thrives on street food. It feeds the masses. If you are looking for a quick lunch, a tasty snack or a refreshing drink, Mumbai has it all. The people are fiercely loyal to their favorite vendors, some of whom have been around for generations. In fact, my friends Lizzie and Amish had a *chai-off*, both taking me to their favorite *chai wallahs* and tutting at the thought of me drinking and enjoying the other's brew. Just for the record, guys, I enjoyed the Indian Stock Exchange *chai* the most!

I sped through the city on the back of my friend's motorbike, weaving between the blacked-out Mercs, rickshaws, carts and sleeping cows to get to the finest street-food vendors. We ate *chaats* and *pakoras* at Chhatrapati Shivaji terminus, and Parsi sweets on Marine Drive, we sampled the various *puris* and *kulfi* from Chowpatty Beach and drank salted *lassis* from clay mugs in the backstreets of Dharavi.

One smoky stand grilled up chunks of paneer and doused them in a super-spicy green chutney. It was fantastic. The slightly chewy, bland paneer was the perfect vehicle for the explosive chutney, absorbing all the flavor and some of the heat. The dish was simple to prepare, overwhelmingly tasty and only took minutes to make.

Grilled Paneer with Mint Chutney SERVES **2** READY IN **10 MINUTES**

For my version of the classic Indian snack, grilled paneer, I have added a little coconut to the chutney, as it works so well with the mint, chili and ground coriander. It also seems to bring all those fresh ingredients together so that their flavors combine into something new. Mr. Paneer Wallah on Uah Kham Murg in sunny Mumbai, I hope I have made you proud.

1 green chili
¼ red onion
2 large handfuls of mint leaves
½ teaspoon ground coriander
1 tomato

1 ounce creamed coconut
½ lemon
5½ ounces paneer
1 tablespoon olive oil
sea salt

CUT THE TOP OFF THE CHILI and roll the chili between your hands to remove the seeds, then put the chili into a mini food processor. Peel the onion and add it to the food processor. Add the mint leaves, followed by the coriander, tomato, coconut and 3 tablespoons water. Season with salt, squeeze in the juice of the lemon and blend until smooth. Pour into a serving bowl, cover and set aside.

HEAT A GRILL PAN over high heat until smoking. Meanwhile, cut the paneer into ½-inch thick pieces and brush each piece with a little oil. Grill 1 to 1½ minutes on each side, or until charred with perfect grill lines. Transfer to a serving plate and serve with the madly green mint chutney.

Fried Chili Corn SERVES **2** READY IN **10 MINUTES**

A few years ago I was in Thailand for New Year's Eve with all the family. We stayed in a beautiful house on Phuket where we were completely spoiled by the fantastic chef, Jitty. Jitty could cook like an angel sent from cooking heaven, and every meal was a complete pleasure to eat. She realized that she had a bunch of very greedy Brits, which opened up the floodgates to snacks throughout the day. Her awesome corn was served with an ice-cold beer by the pool as the sun went down. I can't give you Thai sunsets or a swimming pool, but make this corn, grab a beer and you'll be just as happy.

3¼ cups sunflower oil
9-ounce can whole kernel corn
¼ cup corn starch

1 teaspoon chili powder
1 teaspoon Chinese five-spice powder
sea salt

HEAT THE OIL in a deep pan over high heat. Meanwhile, drain the corn thoroughly in a colander. Pour it into a mixing bowl and add the corn starch, chili powder, Chinese five-spice powder and 1½ tablespoons cold water. Stir everything together well so the corn is completely coated with the corn starch and spices.

USING A SLOTTED SPOON, carefully transfer the corn to the hot oil. Stir, then deep-fry 3 minutes, or until golden and crunchy. Remove from the oil and drain very well on a plate lined with paper towels. Add the corn to serving bowls and season with salt. Serve with ice-cold beer.

NoT QUITE LUNcH

Here are my favorite recipes for a lazy breakfast, early lunch or brunch. They remind me of being on vacation, which is only ever a good thing, when you can get up at your own pace and eat a long, leisurely meal in the early morning. My Baked Eggs with Lentils & Goat Cheese take only 15 minutes to make and are a winner every time. Fantastic Cochin Crab Cakes, flavored with curry leaves and chili, will transport you to the hot, breezy shores of southern India. And my beautifully sweet Villa Dinari Apricots, swollen in orange juice, cinnamon and honey, and served warm with yogurt, can be put together in just 10 minutes. The most time a recipe in this chapter will take to prepare and cook is 25 minutes.

Chorizo & Chili Focaccia SERVES **2** READY IN **10 MINUTES**

This super-fast dish is basically an open sandwich. The chorizo filling does most of the work and the fennel seeds, chili and garlic make it taste even better. Juicy cherry tomatoes, peppery arugula and salty pecorino add all the extra flavors you need to make one heck of a sandwich—and it only takes 10 minutes to prepare and cook.

7-ounce piece of focaccia
1½ tablespoons olive oil, plus extra
  to serve
5½-ounce piece of chorizo

2 garlic cloves
1 teaspoon fennel seeds
¼ teaspoon crushed chili flakes
heaped ⅔ cup cherry tomatoes

1 lemon
2 handfuls of arugula
1 ounce pecorino cheese

PREHEAT THE BROILER to high. Meanwhile, cut the focaccia in half horizontally and carefully scoop out a little of the center from each half using your fingers. Drizzle ½ tablespoon of the oil over both halves and broil 2½ to 3 minutes, or until golden.

WHILE THE FOCACCIA BROILS, slice the chorizo into bite-size pieces. Peel and slice the garlic into thin slivers. Add the remaining oil to a skillet over medium heat and add the chorizo, garlic, fennel seeds and chili flakes. Stir everything together well and cook 3 to 4 minutes, stirring occasionally, until the chorizo starts turning golden at the edges.

CUT THE CHERRY TOMATOES into quarters while the chorizo cooks, then put them into the center of each broiled focaccia half.

PUT THE FOCACCIA onto a cutting board. Cut the lemon in half and squeeze the juice of 1 half into the pan with the chorizo, then stir well. Tip the delicious golden chorizo onto the focaccia, along with all the pan juices. Scatter the focaccia with the arugula and shavings of the cheese. Cut the remaining half lemon into wedges and serve it, along with a bottle of olive oil, at the table alongside the focaccia.

MIGHTY MOSQUES, BRIGHT BLUE BOSPORUS & TURKISH PIZZAS

Istanbul is such a stunning city. It spans both sides of the mighty Bosporus, a strait that marks the divide between Europe and Asia. The European side is home to the beautiful Blue Mosque, the huge minarets of which dwarf the surrounding buildings, and the amazing Grand Bazaar, which is filled with stands selling spices, dried fruits and snacks. A quick boat trip across the sparkling turquoise waters takes you to the Asian side of the city, which has a much more laid-back feel than the majestic European side.

When I took the boat across the river to the Asian side of the city it was the day of a soccer game between Istanbul Buyuk and Ankaraspor. I am pleased to say that Istanbul thrashed them 3 to 0! Food was available everywhere. It was awesome. We wandered around soaking up the atmosphere, sipping ice-cold beer and munching on delicious snacks, such as *kasarli*, a Turkish cheese sandwich, and yummy *simit*, a chewy ring of bread covered in crunchy sesame seeds, as well as tangy fish and onion kebabs.

All the street food was accompanied by little glass shakers filled with blood-red Turkish chili flakes. The chili flakes have a mild, smoky flavor, like a combination of a sun-dried tomato and dried red chili. The rich flavor worked beautifully with all the charcoal-grilled food.

The street food that did it for me the most was *lahmacun*, or Turkish pizza. This fabulous snack, which could thankfully be found all over the city, had a crispy, chewy base that was covered in ground beef or lamb, spices, tomato and herbs. It was always served with those wonderful chili flakes and with wedges of lemon to freshen it up and enhance all those flavors. I fell in love with this snack and am pleased to say that I have made a super-fast version—my Lahmacun Turkish Pizza can be made in just 10 minutes.

Lahmacun—Turkish Pizza SERVES **2** READY IN **10 MINUTES**

1½ tablespoons olive oil
7 ounces ground lamb
2 garlic cloves
½ teaspoon sweet paprika
½ teaspoon ground cumin

¼ teaspoon ground cinnamon
1 lemon
½ tomato
1 tablespoon sun-dried
  tomato paste

2 flour tortillas
1 small handful of mint leaves
1 small handful of parsley leaves
a pinch of crushed chili flakes
sea salt

PREHEAT THE BROILER to high. Meanwhile, place 1 tablespoon of the oil in a large skillet over high heat. Add the lamb and stir well. Peel and crush in the garlic, and add the paprika, cumin and cinnamon to the pan, then season with salt. Squeeze in the juice of ½ lemon and stir-fry 3 to 4 minutes, or until the lamb is cooked through and golden. Remove from the heat and set aside.

SQUEEZE THE SEEDS out of the tomato half, then finely chop the flesh. Add the tomato to the cooked lamb followed by the sun-dried tomato paste. Stir well.

PUT THE TORTILLAS onto a broiler rack and brush with the remaining oil. Spoon the spicy lamb onto the tortillas and broil 1 to 2 minutes, or until the tortillas start to get crisp at the edges.

WHILE THE LAHMACUN COOKS, finely chop the herbs and cut the remaining lemon half into quarters. Scatter the herbs and chili flakes onto the cooked lahmacun and serve with the lemon wedges on the side.

Cochin Crab Cakes SERVES **2** READY IN **15 MINUTES**

My Cochin Crab Cakes make the perfect light meal. They are packed with juicy crabmeat, and with tomatoes, cilantro and scallions to freshen things up. Finally, mustard seeds, curry leaves, turmeric and chili add the flavors of southern India. The hit of lime at the end accentuates all the spices even more, so in only 15 minutes you get something amazing.

2 tablespoons peanut oil
1 teaspoon mustard seeds
a large pinch of dried curry leaves
¼ teaspoon turmeric
¼ teaspoon chili powder
3 scallions
5 cherry tomatoes

1 handful of cilantro leaves
1½ cups cooked white crabmeat
¾ cup fresh breadcrumbs
1 small egg
1 lime
sea salt

ADD 1 TABLESPOON OF THE OIL to a small skillet over medium heat and then add the mustard seeds. Fry 30 seconds, shaking the pan continuously, or until the mustard seeds start popping. Rub the curry leaves between your hands to break them up and let them drop into the pan. Remove the pan from the heat and add the turmeric and chili powder, and set aside.

TRIM THE SCALLIONS, then finely chop them with the cherry tomatoes and cilantro, and add them all to a mixing bowl. Pour in the crabmeat and breadcrumbs, and season with salt. Add the cooked spices and oil from the skillet, then crack in the egg and stir everything together well to combine. Divide the mixture into 4 and flatten each one into a crab cake about ½ inch thick.

ADD THE REMAINING OIL to a large skillet over medium heat and fry the crab cakes 2 minutes on each side, or until beautifully golden and warmed through. Cut the lime into wedges and serve with the hot crab cakes.

Shrimp Tortas with Salsa Mexicana SERVES 2 READY IN 20 MINUTES

FOR THE SHRIMP TORTAS
7 ounces potatoes
1 garlic clove
4 scallions
1 handful of cilantro leaves
6 ounces raw shelled jumbo shrimp
1 ounce feta cheese

½ egg
scant ⅔ cup all-purpose flour
1 tablespoon olive oil, plus extra
  for greasing
sea salt and freshly ground black
  pepper

FOR THE SALSA MEXICANA
1 garlic clove
⅔ cup drained sun-dried tomatoes
  in oil
1 dried chipotle chili
1 tablespoon olive oil
½ lime

CHOP THE UNPEELED POTATOES into ½-inch cubes and cook them in a saucepan of boiling water 8 minutes, or until tender. Drain in a colander and refresh under cold water, then drain again. Return the potatoes to the saucepan and lightly mash them so they start to break down. Set aside.

WHILE THE POTATOES COOK, peel the garlic and trim the scallions, then put them into a food processor with the cilantro and blend to roughly chop. Add the shrimp and feta cheese, and blend to a rough paste. Pour the paste into a large mixing bowl, add the egg and flour, then season with salt and pepper. Transfer the mashed potatoes to the bowl and stir everything together well until it has a doughlike consistency.

ADD THE OIL to a small skillet over high heat. Scoop the potato mixture into the pan and spread it out to cover the base. Reduce the heat to medium and cook 1½ to 2 minutes, shaking the pan occasionally, until golden on one side.

MEANWHILE, TO MAKE THE SALSA, peel the garlic, then put it into a mini food processor or blender along with the sun-dried tomatoes, chili and oil. Squeeze in the juice of the lime, season with salt and blend to a smooth paste. Pour the smoky salsa into a serving bowl and set aside.

WHEN THE TORTAS HAS COOKED on one side, rub a little oil onto a side plate and carefully place it, oil-side down, over the pan with the half-cooked tortas. Holding the plate and the skillet handle, carefully flip the skillet over so that the tortas rests on the plate. Slip it back into the skillet and cook another 1½ to 2 minutes, or until golden. Serve with the hot, smoky salsa on the side.

Baked Eggs with Lentils
& Goat Cheese SERVES **2** READY IN **15 MINUTES**

At the moment, baked eggs are very trendy, and for good reason—they are delicious and require little effort. My baked eggs sit on a bed of lentils, sage, chili and scallions. I have added sun-dried tomato paste and paprika to introduce even more flavor without taking up any extra time. A final crumble of salty goat cheese, which melts into the eggs while they finish cooking, finishes everything off perfectly.

1 garlic clove
3 scallions
½ red chili
8 sage leaves
2 tablespoons olive oil

15-ounce can green lentils
scant ⅔ cup tomato
  passata
1 tablespoon sun-dried
  tomato paste
2 eggs

2 ounces goat cheese
¼ teaspoon paprika
2 slices of fantastic bread
sea salt and freshly
  ground black pepper

PREHEAT THE BROILER to high. Meanwhile, peel the garlic and trim the scallions, then finely chop the garlic, scallions, chili and sage. Place 1 tablespoon of the oil in a large ovenproof skillet over medium heat and add the chopped ingredients. Cook 3 to 4 minutes, stirring occasionally, until the scallions have started to soften.

DRAIN AND RINSE THE LENTILS, then pour them into the pan. Add the passata and sun-dried tomato paste, then season with a good pinch of salt and pepper. Stir everything together really well to combine.

MAKE TWO SHALLOW WELLS in the lentil mixture and crack in the eggs. Crumble the goat cheese over the top and put a small pinch of paprika and salt onto each egg. Broil 4 to 5 minutes, or until the egg whites have just set but the yolks are still runny.

PUT THE BREAD INTO THE TOASTER to toast while the eggs cook. Drizzle the remaining oil over the cooked eggs and serve with the toast.

Parsi Eggs SERVES **2** READY IN **15 MINUTES**

This was my breakfast in a little Parsi café in Mumbai after a long overnight train journey from Goa. The eggs were Indianed up with loads of spices and mixed with vegetables and fresh cilantro. It was the perfect start to the day in that magnificent city.

4 eggs
¼ teaspoon chili powder
½ teaspoon ground coriander
¼ teaspoon garam masala
1 garlic clove
3 scallions
1 tomato

1 handful of cilantro leaves
2 slices of brown bread
1 tablespoon olive oil
heaped ⅓ cup frozen peas
heaped ⅓ cup canned kernel corn
sea salt

CRACK THE EGGS into a mixing bowl and add the chili powder, ground coriander and garam masala. Season with a good pinch of salt and beat together. Set aside.

PEEL THE GARLIC and trim the scallions, then finely chop the garlic, scallions, tomato and cilantro leaves. Set aside with the cilantro in a separate pile. Put the bread in the toaster to toast while you cook the eggs.

ADD THE OIL to a large skillet over high heat, then add the garlic, scallions and tomato. Stir-fry the mixture 2 minutes, or until the tomato starts to break down and become a little dry.

POUR IN THE PEAS and kernel corn, then mix well. Reduce the heat to medium and add the egg mixture. Stir everything together really well and let sit 1 minute to set. Add the cilantro and cook 1 to 2 minutes, stirring continuously, until set. Serve with the toast.

Blue Mosque Goat Cheese Tart SERVES 2 READY IN **25 MINUTES**

My goat cheese tart is a twist on the classic Turkish snack borek. I have made one large tart instead of fiddly individual portions, and stuffed it with chili, scallions, olives, walnuts, tarragon, goat cheese and paprika.

1 green chili
3 scallions
scant ⅓ cup pitted green olives
scant ½ cup walnuts
1 large handful of tarragon leaves

4½ ounces soft goat cheese
¼ teaspoon paprika
1 lemon
2 tablespoons olive oil

3 sheets of filo pastry, defrosted
  if frozen
heaped ⅓ cup yogurt
sea salt and freshly ground black
  pepper

PREHEAT THE OVEN to 350°F. Cut the top off the chili and roll the chili between your hands to remove the seeds. Trim the scallions. Put the chili and scallions into a food processor, and add the olives, walnuts and tarragon. Blend until coarsely chopped, then add the goat cheese and paprika. Squeeze in the juice of ½ lemon and season with salt and pepper. Give it a quick blast to mix it all together.

TAKE A PIECE OF PARCHMENT PAPER large enough to fit in a baking pan, and crumple it up using your hands (this stops the sides from curling up). Flatten the parchment paper onto a cutting board and brush with olive oil. Lay a piece of the filo pastry on top of the parchment paper and brush it all over with oil (cover the unused filo with a damp dish towel to prevent it from drying out). Put another piece of filo pastry on top of the first layer and brush it with oil.

SCOOP THE FILLING into the center of the pastry and spread it out into a rectangular shape about ⅝ inch thick. Cover with the final sheet of filo pastry and fold in the sides to form a neat rectangle. Brush the top of the tart with oil and season with salt and pepper.

TRANSFER THE TART to the baking pan by lifting up the sides of the parchment paper, then bake 15 to 18 minutes, or until golden on top. Meanwhile, put the yogurt into a serving bowl, squeeze in the juice of the remaining ½ lemon and season with salt and pepper. Mix well. Serve the hot tart with the lemony yogurt on the side.

Za'atar Halloumi with Couscous Salad SERVES 2 READY IN 15 MINUTES

FOR THE ZA'ATAR HALLOUMI
1 tablespoon sumac
1 tablespoon dried oregano
3 teaspoons sesame seeds
7 ounces halloumi
2 tablespoons olive oil

FOR THE COUSCOUS
⅓ cup couscous
1 red chili
1 handful of parsley leaves
1 tablespoon capers
1 tablespoon olive oil

½ lemon
sea salt and freshly ground
   black pepper

TO MAKE THE ZA'ATAR, mix the sumac, oregano, sesame seeds and a good pinch of salt in a bowl.

PUT HALF THE ZA'ATAR into a large mixing bowl, add the couscous and stir with a fork to combine. Pour in a generous ⅓ cup warm water, cover with plastic wrap and set aside to allow the couscous to absorb the water. This will take about 10 minutes.

MEANWHILE, CUT THE TOP off the chili and roll the chili between your hands to remove the seeds, then finely chop the chili and parsley. Drain and finely chop the capers. Set aside.

CUT THE HALLOUMI into ¼-inch slices and press each piece into the za'atar spices to cover with a thin layer on one side. Heat the oil in large skillet over medium heat. Add the halloumi, spice-side down, and fry 2 to 3 minutes on each side until golden. Remove the pan from the heat and set it aside while you finish making the salad.

WHEN THE COUSCOUS has absorbed all the water, fluff it up with a fork, then add the olive oil and squeeze in the juice of the lemon. Stir in the chopped chili, parsley and capers, and add a pinch of salt, if needed, and pepper. Serve the couscous with the delicious fried halloumi.

Orange & Cardamom French Toast SERVES **2** READY IN **15 MINUTES**

For those with a sweet tooth, my Orange & Cardamom French Toast won't disappoint. The toast is cooked until crisp in a mixture of butter, cardamom, golden raisins and orange. The cardamom flavors everything, and the golden raisins swell up in the perfumed juices. I use maple syrup as the crowning glory, because I love the slightly smoky sweetness it gives to the overall flavour of the dish.

2 eggs
scant ½ cup milk
1 orange
1 tablespoon powdered sugar
4 thick slices of white bread
 (about ½ inch thick)

2 heaped tablespoons butter
scant ½ cup golden raisins
6 cardamom pods
3 tablespoons maple syrup

CRACK THE EGGS into a mixing bowl and pour in the milk. Add the zest of the orange to the bowl followed by the powdered sugar and beat together. Place the bread in a shallow dish and pour the egg mixture over it. Ensure that both sides of each slice of bread are well soaked so that nearly all the liquid is absorbed. Set aside.

PUT THE BUTTER and golden raisins into a large skillet over medium heat. Gently crush the cardamom pods by pressing down on them with the flat side of a knife blade, then add them to the butter. Quarter the orange and squeeze the juice of one quarter into the skillet. Stir well and cook gently 1 minute, or until the butter melts.

ADD THE BREAD to the skillet and fry 2½ to 3 minutes on each side until beautifully golden, shaking the pan occasionally. Divide between two serving plates and squeeze the juice of the remaining orange quarters onto each piece of toast. Drizzle with the maple syrup and serve with the yummy golden raisins.

Villa Dinari Apricots with Yogurt SERVES **2**   READY IN **10 MINUTES**

During my time in Morocco I cooked dinner with the chefs at the beautiful Villa Dinari. We made a feast that included a particularly wonderful lamb and pear tagine, which was finished off with dried apricots that had been cooked slowly in sugar and cinnamon. They were fantastic. I thought that the apricots, with a little twist, would be excellent added to a big fat bowl of creamy yogurt. For my fast breakfast version I cook the apricots for a couple of minutes in butter, orange, cinnamon and honey. Once they have swollen to capacity they go straight into bowls to be topped with some yogurt and a scattering of crunchy walnuts.

2 tablespoons butter
generous ¾ cup ready-to-eat
   dried apricots
½ teaspoon ground cinnamon

2 tablespoons honey
½ orange
1 cup yogurt
scant ½ cup walnuts

PLACE THE BUTTER in a skillet over medium heat and add the apricots, cinnamon and honey.

SQUEEZE IN THE JUICE of the orange and stir well. Cook 5 to 6 minutes, stirring occasionally, until the apricots have swollen and the sauce has thickened. Spoon the apricots and the lovely sticky sauce into two serving bowls. Divide the yogurt among the two bowls and scatter each with walnuts to serve.

MIDWEEK LIFESAVERS

My midweek lifesavers are all you need to know for those crucial moments in life when you get in late from work and want to eat immediately. With no messing around required, these recipes are fast, fresh and furious. Try my heavenly Cambodian Seafood Amok, a coconut curry that can be made in just 15 minutes, or my Little South Island Pork Salad, which is made with juicy orange pieces and crunchy fennel, flavored with Chinese five-spice powder and chili flakes. This chapter is also home to the mighty Bosporus Burger, a succulent beef burger flavored with spices and served with blue cheese. This epic creation takes only 15 minutes to make, so you'll never be caught out hungry again. Most recipes in this chapter take 20 minutes or less to prepare and the longest takes only 25 minutes.

Goan Cinnamon & Mint Chicken Curry SERVES **2** READY IN **20 MINUTES**

This classic Goan dish is one of my favorite curries ever. It's vibrant in color and fresh tasting, but the best thing is that it's so simple to make. Add everything to a blender to make a killer sauce, fry the chicken, pour in the sauce and cook for a few minutes. What could be simpler?

scant ⅔ cup basmati rice
2 green chilies
3 garlic cloves
2 large handfuls of cilantro leaves and stalks
1 large handful of mint leaves

½ teaspoon ground cinnamon
½ teaspoon freshly ground black pepper
1 teaspoon sugar
1½ teaspoons Worcestershire sauce
½-inch piece fresh gingerroot

1 lime
10½ ounces boneless, skinless chicken thighs
1 tablespoon peanut oil
sea salt

COOK THE RICE in boiling water 10 to 12 minutes, or until soft, or following directions on the package. Drain in a strainer, then cover the rice with a clean dish towel while still in the strainer, and set aside.

MEANWHILE, CUT THE TOP off each chili and roll the chili between your hands to remove the seeds, then add the chilies to a blender or food processor. Peel the garlic and add it to the blender with the cilantro leaves and stalks, mint, cinnamon, black pepper, sugar, Worcestershire sauce and a good pinch of salt. Peel and add the ginger, then squeeze in the juice of the lime and add a scant ½ cup water. Blend until smooth.

SLICE THE CHICKEN into thin strips. Add the oil to a skillet over high heat. Then add the chicken and stir-fry 5 to 6 minutes, or until it starts to turn golden brown. Pour in the green sauce and reduce the heat to medium. Add a scant ½ cup water to the blender, swill it around and add it to the pan to get every last drop of sauce into the dish. Stir everything together really well and simmer 5 to 6 minutes, stirring occasionally, until the chicken is cooked through and tender. Serve with the rice.

Phipp Street Stir-Fry SERVES **2** READY IN **15 MINUTES**

I live on Phipp Street, in London, and this stir-fry was invented after a long day working in my kitchen. I mine-swept my almost empty fridge, chopped everything up and stir-fried it with some noodles. The result was this awesome dish. I hope it brings you as much satisfaction as it did me when you need a good feed after a long day and have little time for cooking.

5 ounces vermicelli rice noodles
2 tablespoons peanut oil
2 lemongrass stalks
2 garlic cloves
1 red chili
1 baby gem lettuce

2 boneless, skinless chicken thighs
   (7 ounces total weight)
2 teaspoons fish sauce
1 tablespoon light soy sauce
½ lime

COOK THE NOODLES in boiling water 2 to 3 minutes, or until soft, or following directions on the package. Drain in a strainer and drizzle with 1 tablespoon of the oil to prevent the noodles from sticking together, then set aside.

MEANWHILE, GET EVERYTHING READY to stir-fry. Remove the tough outer leaves from the lemongrass and cut off the ends of the stalks. Peel the garlic and cut the top off the chili, then add the lemongrass, garlic and chili to a mini food processor, and blend to a paste. Cut the stalk off the lettuce, separate the leaves and set aside. Slice the chicken into very thin strips and reserve.

HEAT THE REMAINING OIL in a wok over high heat until smoking. Add the chicken and stir-fry 5 to 6 minutes, or until golden at the edges. Scoop the spice paste into the wok and stir-fry another 30 seconds, or until fragrant. Add the lettuce leaves, fish sauce and soy sauce, then squeeze in the juice of the lime. Stir-fry 1 to 2 minutes, or until the lettuce leaves have wilted and the chicken is cooked through. Finally, add the noodles, toss everything together and serve.

Chicken Morita with Avocado Sauce SERVES **2** READY IN **20 MINUTES**

FOR THE CHICKEN MORITA
scant ⅔ cup basmati rice
2 garlic cloves
1 teaspoon smoked paprika
½ teaspoon chili powder
2 tablespoons sun-dried
   tomato paste

1 teaspoon tamarind paste
¼ teaspoon sugar
2 tablespoons olive oil
2 skinless chicken breasts
sea salt

FOR THE AVOCADO SAUCE
1 avocado
1 lime
heaped ⅓ cup yogurt
1 small handful of cilantro leaves

PREHEAT THE BROILER to high. Cook the rice in boiling water 10 to 12 minutes, or until soft, or following directions on the package. Drain in a strainer, cover the rice with a clean dish towel while still in the strainer and set aside.

MEANWHILE, PEEL THE GARLIC, then put it into a mini food processor, and add the paprika, chili powder, sun-dried tomato paste, tamarind paste, sugar, 1 tablespoon of the olive oil and a good pinch of salt, and blend until smooth.

LAY THE CHICKEN BREASTS on a cutting board and, using a rolling pin, bash them out until they are about ⅝ inch thick. Prick the chicken all over with a fork, then rub the paste all over both sides. Put the chicken onto a broiler rack and broil 7 to 8 minutes, or until golden on one side.

WHILE THE CHICKEN BROILS, cut the avocado in half and remove the seed using a knife. Scoop the flesh out with a spoon and put it into a blender or food processor. Squeeze in the juice of ½ lime and add the yogurt, cilantro, the remaining oil and a good pinch of salt. Blend until smooth, then pour into a serving bowl. Cover and set aside. Cut the remaining lime half into 2 wedges.

TURN THE HALF-COOKED CHICKEN over and broil another 7 to 8 minutes, or until cooked through and tender. Serve the chicken with a wedge of lime and the cooked rice, and add the avocado sauce at the table.

Great Eastern Duck Salad SERVES **2** READY IN **25 MINUTES**

1 tablespoon olive oil
2 duck breasts
 (about 5¾ ounces each)
¾-pound watermelon
½ red chili
½ lime
2 tablespoons hoisin sauce

1 teaspoon light soy sauce
¼ teaspoon Chinese five-spice
 powder
2½ cups watercress
1 handful of mint leaves
heaped ⅓ cup cashews
sea salt

HEAT THE OIL in a skillet over high heat. Meanwhile, score the fat on the duck breasts and season both sides with salt. Carefully put the duck in the hot pan, skin-side down, and reduce the heat to medium. Cook 8 to 10 minutes, or until the skin is really crisp.

WHILE THE DUCK COOKS, scoop the watermelon out of the shell and cut the flesh into bite-size pieces, removing any large seeds. Add the watermelon pieces to a large mixing bowl and set aside.

TURN THE CRISPY DUCK over and cook another 8 to 10 minutes, or until beautifully tender and pink in the center, then remove from the heat.

SEED AND FINELY SLICE THE CHILI while the duck finishes cooking. Add it to the mixing bowl with the watermelon and squeeze in the juice of the lime.

POUR AWAY ANY EXCESS FAT from the cooked duck. Add the hoisin sauce, soy sauce and Chinese five-spice powder to the pan, and mix well. Remove the duck breasts from the pan, slice them into thick pieces and set aside. Add the watercress, mint and cashews to the bowl with the watermelon and toss everything together. Serve the salad with the beautiful duck slices, with the pan juices spooned on top.

Oaxaca Tostadas SERVES **2** READY IN **15 MINUTES**

My *tostadas* were inspired by the wonderful giant *tostadas* of the Central Market in the city of Oaxaca in Mexico. They are completely delicious—you taste hot and cold, crunchy and smooth, spicy and mild, salty and sour in every bite. And, because they only take 15 minutes to make, they are a real midweek lifesaver.

2 tablespoons olive oil
2 large tortillas
1 red onion
2 garlic cloves
7-ounce piece of chorizo

2 ripe avocados
1 green chili
8 scallions
1 handful of cilantro leaves
1½ limes

1 tomato
2 ounces Gruyère cheese
a pinch of smoked paprika
sea salt

PREHEAT THE BROILER TO HIGH. Meanwhile, brush 1 tablespoon of the oil all over both sides of each tortilla. Put them onto a broiler rack and broil 30 seconds to 1 minute on each side, or until crisp and golden at the edges. Remove from the broiler and place on serving plates.

PEEL THE RED ONION AND GARLIC, then slice the onion and roughly chop the garlic and chorizo. Heat the remaining oil in a skillet over medium heat and add the sliced and chopped ingredients. Stir well and cook 5 to 6 minutes, stirring occasionally, until golden.

MEANWHILE, CUT THE AVOCADOS in half and remove the seeds using a knife. Scoop the flesh out with a spoon and put it into a mini food processor or blender. Cut the top off the chili and trim the scallions, then add both ingredients to the food processor with the cilantro and a pinch of salt. Squeeze in the juice of ½ lime and blend to a rough paste.

FINELY SLICE THE TOMATO, grate the cheese and quarter the remaining lime. Divide the avocado mixture among the 2 tortillas and spread it evenly over them, using a knife. Arrange the tomato slices, hot chorizo and onion on top, and scatter with the cheese. Dust both tostadas with smoked paprika and serve with the lime quarters.

TINY TABLES, MOTORBIKES & BUN CHA

When I arrived in Hanoi I was struck by the madness of the place. The air was sticky, people actually wore conical hats, smoky food stands lined the streets and an army of predatory motorbikes circled the roads like angry bulls at Pamplona.

Once I had plucked up the courage to cross a road (which was only after watching an old lady fearlessly stride to the other side), I was able to sample the many culinary delights of the city. Perfectly barbecued meats, grilled fish, peppered stir-fries and fragrant soups—Hanoi had it all, with fishy, hot, salty and sour flavors beautifully balanced in every bite.

Eating in Hanoi means eating street food—and it was everywhere. A few stands had evolved into restaurants, but on the whole you eat out on the curb, crouched at tiny tables. One lunchtime, I visited a packed street stand and squeezed onto a tiny chair, literally in the road, to slurp the lunchtime soup special, *bun cha*. It was amazing! The wonderfully salty soup was spiked with black pepper and served with tender grilled pork. The table came laden with little dishes of rice noodles, herbs and chilies to add to your bowl. This fast-food glory summed up all that was triumphant about Vietnamese food.

Vietnamese Bun Cha SERVES **2** READY IN **20 MINUTES**

FOR THE SOUP
2 cups chicken stock
6 black peppercorns
2 star anise
1-inch stick of cinnamon
2 teaspoons sugar
3 tablespoons fish sauce
2 lemongrass stalks

½ lime
5 ounces vermicelli rice noodles

FOR THE PORK PATTIES
1 small handful of cilantro leaves
1 small handful of mint leaves
4¼ ounces ground pork
1 teaspoon fish sauce
1 teaspoon peanut oil

TO SERVE
4 scallions
½ red chili
½ lime
1½ cups bean sprouts
1 large handful of cilantro leaves
1 large handful of mint leaves

POUR THE STOCK and 2 cups water into a saucepan and add the peppercorns, star anise, cinnamon stick, sugar and fish sauce. Bash the fat ends of the lemongrass stalks with a spoon, snap them in half and add them to the pan. Squeeze in the juice of the lime, stir well and bring to a boil over medium heat.

MEANWHILE, ADD THE NOODLES to a pan of boiling water and let stand 3 minutes, or following the directions on the package. Drain in a strainer and refresh under cold water, then drain again. Set aside to continue draining in the strainer.

CHOP THE HERBS for the pork patties and put them into a large bowl. Add the pork and fish sauce and stir well to combine. Heat the oil in a skillet over medium heat. Meanwhile, divide the pork into 4 and flatten into mini burger patties. Fry the patties 3 minutes on each side, or until golden and cooked through.

WHILE THE PORK IS COOKING, trim the scallions, then cut each in half and then into thin strips. Seed the chili, then slice it finely. Cut the lime in half.

DIVIDE THE NOODLES and bean sprouts among two large serving bowls, and put 2 pork patties into each bowl. Scatter each bowl with half the scallions and the chili, then top with the lime and the herbs. Remove the spices from the stock and divide the hot, fragrant soup among the two bowls. Serve immediately.

Little South Island Pork Salad SERVES **2** READY IN **20 MINUTES**

This dish sums up why eating real Chinese food is such a pleasure. No radioactive-red gloopy sauce, not a canned pineapple chunk in sight—just simple, fresh, clean flavors that all work superbly together in a dish that takes minutes to make. The crunchy fennel and sweet carrot soak up all the richness of the stir-fried pork and the delicious flavors of the tart dressing. This is how Chinese food should be!

FOR THE PORK SALAD
1 tablespoon peanut oil
¾ pound ground pork
½ teaspoon Chinese five-spice
  powder
½ teaspoon crushed chili flakes

1 tablespoon light soy sauce
1 orange
1 fennel bulb
1 carrot
3½ ounces frisée lettuce leaves

FOR THE GINGER DRESSING
1½ tablespoons cider vinegar
2 teaspoons light soy sauce
½ inch piece fresh gingerroot

HEAT A WOK over high heat until smoking. Pour in the oil, swirl it around and then add the pork. Stir-fry 5 to 6 minutes, or until the edges of the pork start to catch and become golden.

SPRINKLE THE CHINESE FIVE-SPICE POWDER and chili flakes onto the pork and add the soy sauce. Continue to stir-fry 30 seconds, then remove from the heat and set aside.

USING A SHARP KNIFE, cut the top and bottom off the orange, and stand it up on your cutting board. Carefully slice the skin off in sections, cutting from top to bottom. Remove any remaining pith, then cut the juicy pieces of orange away from the membrane and put them in a mixing bowl. Squeeze in any juices from the membrane.

FINELY SLICE THE FENNEL and add it to the bowl with the orange. Peel the carrot and grate it, using the coarse setting on a grater, into the bowl. Pour in the cider vinegar and soy sauce for the dressing, then peel and finely grate in the ginger. Add the lettuce leaves and cooked pork, along with all the lovely juices, into the mixing bowl and toss everything together to serve.

Mr. Wong's Hunan Lamb SERVES **2** READY IN **20 MINUTES**

This dish is all about the big spices of Hunanese cooking. A fiery paste made from dried chilies, Szechuan pepper, ginger and scallions is used to coat the delicate lamb cutlets and turns them into something fierce. The sweetness of the lamb handles all the big flavors, and the delicate bok choy, soy and orange stir-fry absorbs some of the heat.

FOR THE LAMB
2 dried red chilies
1 teaspoon Szechuan pepper
½-inch piece fresh gingerroot
5 scallions

2 tablespoons peanut oil
6 lamb cutlets (about
   1 pound 2 ounces total weight)
sea salt

**FOR THE BOK CHOY AND
   ORANGE STIR-FRY**
7 ounces bok choy
1 tablespoon peanut oil
1 tablespoon soy sauce
½ orange

PREHEAT THE BROILER to high. Meanwhile, put the chilies, Szechuan pepper and a pinch of salt into a mini food processor, and blend to a coarse powder. Peel the ginger and trim the scallions, then add them to the food processor, followed by the oil. Blend to a rough paste.

LIGHTLY SCORE both sides of the lamb cutlets in a criss-cross pattern and put them in a mixing bowl. Pour in the spice paste and mix everything together well so the paste completely covers the lamb. Put the lamb on a broiler rack and broil 5 to 6 minutes on each side, or until golden outside and pink and juicy in the center.

WHILE THE LAMB COOKS, cut the bok choy lengthwise into quarters. Place a wok over high heat until smoking and pour in the oil. Add the bok choy and stir-fry 2 minutes, then add the soy sauce and squeeze in the juice of the orange. Continue to stir-fry 30 seconds, then reduce the heat to low and cook 3 to 4 minutes, or until tender. Serve the stir-fry with the lamb.

Grilled Eggplant with Lamb, Mint & Feta SERVES **2**   READY IN **15 MINUTES**

This is my express version of a classic Eastern Mediterranean stuffed-eggplant dish. I grill the eggplant, which is the fastest way to cook it, and top it with stir-fried lamb. The final addition of mint and feta completes the dish with the fresh and salty flavors it needs.

1 large eggplant
3 tablespoons olive oil
2 bay leaves
10½ ounces ground lamb
1¼ teaspoons ground allspice

½ teaspoon ground cinnamon
2 garlic cloves
scant 1¼ cups tomato passata
2¼ ounces feta cheese
1 small handful of mint leaves

sea salt and freshly ground
 black pepper

TO SERVE
green salad

HEAT A GRILL PAN over high heat until smoking. Meanwhile, cut the eggplant lengthwise into ½-inch slices and add them to a mixing bowl. Add 2 tablespoons of the oil and a good pinch of salt and pepper. Mix everything together really well so that both sides of the eggplant slices are coated in the oil. Cook 2½ to 3 minutes on each side, or until charred and tender. Divide between two serving plates and set aside.

WHILE THE EGGPLANT COOKS, add the remaining oil to a skillet over medium heat. Add the bay leaves and cook 5 seconds until fragrant. Add the lamb, allspice, cinnamon and a good pinch of salt and pepper. Peel and crush in the garlic, turn the heat up to high and stir-fry 3 to 4 minutes, or until the lamb is golden.

POUR IN THE PASSATA and mix well. Reduce the heat to medium and cook 3 to 4 minutes, stirring occasionally, until the lamb is cooked through and the sauce has thickened. To serve the dish, spoon the lamb onto the grilled eggplant slices. Scatter with crumbled feta cheese and the mint leaves and serve with a green salad.

Taiwanese Beef Noodle Stir-Fry SERVES **2** READY IN **15 MINUTES**

5 ounces medium egg noodles
2½ tablespoons peanut oil
8-ounce sirloin steak
1 red chili
4 scallions
4 garlic cloves

¼-inch piece fresh gingerroot
1 heaped cup snow peas
½ teaspoon freshly ground black
  pepper
½ teaspoon sugar
2 tablespoons soy sauce

COOK THE NOODLES in boiling water 4 to 5 minutes until soft, or following directions on the package. Drain in a strainer and drizzle with 1 tablespoon of the oil to prevent the noodles from sticking together. Using a pair of scissors, cut the noodles a few at a time to shorten them (this will help them mix quicker in the wok). Set aside.

MEANWHILE, PREPARE ALL THE INGREDIENTS for the stir-fry. Finely slice the beef into very thin strips. Cut the top off the chili, then finely slice the chili. Trim the scallions and cut into 1-inch pieces. Peel and cut the garlic cloves in half lengthwise. Peel the ginger, then slice it into thin strips.

HEAT A WOK over high heat until smoking. Pour in the remaining oil and add the chili, scallions, garlic and ginger, then stir-fry 30 seconds until beautifully aromatic. Add the beef and continue to stir-fry 2 minutes, then add the snow peas, black pepper and sugar.

CONTINUE TO STIR-FRY 1 to 2 minutes, or until everything has taken on a lovely golden color and the beef is cooked through. Transfer the cooked noodles to the hot wok and pour in the soy sauce. Toss everything well and serve.

Beef Chili & Mint Stir-Fry SERVES **2** READY IN **15 MINUTES**

Never one to miss a meal, I ordered my lunch to go as I was leaving my hotel in Laos to head to the airport and back to Blighty. I was eating my food as I walked to the taxi. Boy, am I glad that I am greedy. Lunch was superb—a simple beef stir-fry with chili, garlic and a few peanuts, which was lifted somewhere new with a handful of mint leaves. The mint was a superb addition to a classic southeastern Asian stir-fry and probably even worth missing a flight for.

5 ounces fine egg noodles
2½ tablespoons peanut oil
2 garlic cloves
1-inch piece fresh gingerroot
1 red chili

2 sirloin steaks
 (about 4¼ ounces each)
heaped ⅓ cup peanuts
1 teaspoon rice wine vinegar
1 tablespoon light soy sauce

3 tablespoons oyster sauce
1⅔ cups bean sprouts
1 handful of small mint leaves

COOK THE NOODLES in boiling water 4 to 5 minutes, or until soft, or following directions on the package. Drain in a strainer and drizzle with ½ tablespoon of the oil to prevent the noodles from sticking together, then set aside. Meanwhile, peel and finely slice the garlic and ginger. Cut the top off the chili, then slice the chili. Trim and discard any fat off the steak and slice the meat into strips about 1/16 inch thick.

HEAT A WOK over high heat and add 1 tablespoon of the oil. Add the peanuts and stir-fry 1 minute, or until golden. Remove with a slotted spoon and transfer to a plate lined with paper towels to drain. Pour away and discard the oil remaining in the wok. Return the wok to high heat and, when smoking hot, add the remaining oil and the sliced steak. Let sear 40 seconds, then stir-fry 30 seconds to take on some color. Add the garlic, ginger and chili, and continue to stir-fry 2 to 3 minutes, or until the garlic is golden.

POUR IN THE RICE WINE VINEGAR, soy sauce and oyster sauce, and stir well. Add the bean sprouts and continue to stir-fry 1 to 2 minutes, or until the bean sprouts are just tender but still have a little bite. Turn off the heat, then add the peanuts and the mint. Give it a final stir, then add the noodles, toss to combine and serve.

The Bosporus Burger SERVES **2** READY IN **15 MINUTES**

1 small handful of parsley leaves
1 teaspoon paprika
2 teaspoons ground cumin
½ teaspoon ground ginger
½ teaspoon chili powder
10½ ounces ground beef
1 tablespoon olive oil

2 ounces blue cheese
¼ cup mayonnaise
¼ lemon
2 hamburger buns
a few large lettuce leaves
sea salt

FINELY CHOP THE PARSLEY and add it to a large mixing bowl. Add the paprika, cumin, ground ginger, chili powder, ground beef and a really good pinch of salt. Mix everything together really well—I find that squeezing the mixture together using your hands works best.

DIVIDE THE BEEF MIXTURE into 2 portions and flatten each one into a patty. Push your thumb into the top of each patty to create a little indentation, which will help them cook evenly.

HEAT THE OIL in a skillet over high heat and add the patties, indented-side facing up. Cook 4 minutes, then turn the patties over, reduce the heat to medium-low and cook another 3 minutes. Place half of the blue cheese on each patty and cook 1 minute, or until the patties have cooked through and are wonderfully juicy and the cheese has just melted.

WHILE THE PATTIES COOK, put the mayonnaise in a mixing bowl and squeeze in the juice of the lemon. Add a pinch of salt and mix well. Split the hamburger buns in half and spread each evenly with the mayonnaise. Divide the lettuce leaves among the buns. Place the cooked beef patties on top of the lettuce, put the lid of the buns on top and tuck in immediately.

Salmon Bibimbap SERVES **2**   READY IN **20 MINUTES**

Bibimbap is a classic Korean rice dish. Cooked rice is put into a boiling-hot stone bowl where it forms a crunchy crust. Different toppings—salmon, eggs, vegetables or pork—are added, and the dish is served with kimchi and a soy-based sauce. When you cook my salmon version ensure that the pan is really hot before you add the cooked rice so you get a good crispy crust.

FOR THE RICE
scant ⅔ cup jasmine rice
½-inch piece fresh gingerroot
3 scallions
1 tablespoon light soy sauce
1 tablespoon cider vinegar

FOR THE SALMON AND EGGS
2 tablespoons olive oil
2 boneless, skinless salmon fillets
2 eggs
1 teaspoon sesame seeds

FOR THE CHILI DRESSING
1 garlic clove
¼ cup chili sauce
1 tablespoon soy sauce
1 tablespoon cider vinegar
1 teaspoon sesame oil

COOK THE RICE in boiling water 10 to 12 minutes, or until soft, or following directions on the package. Drain in a strainer, return to the pan, then cover and set aside. Meanwhile, heat 1 tablespoon of the oil for the salmon in a skillet over medium heat and add the salmon. Cook 2 minutes, then turn, reduce the heat to low and cook 1½ to 2 minutes, or until cooked on the outside and pink in the center. Set aside.

WHILE THE SALMON COOKS, peel the garlic for the dressing. Put all the dressing ingredients into a mini food processor and blend until smooth. Set aside.

PEEL THE GINGER for the rice and trim the scallions, then finely chop them both and add them to the pan with the cooked rice. Add the soy sauce and cider vinegar, then stir together to combine using a fork. Cover and set aside.

HEAT THE REMAINING OIL in a large skillet over high heat and add the rice, spreading it evenly. Then, using a spoon, create two wells and crack in the eggs. Cover and cook 2 to 3 minutes, or until the whites have set, the yolks are runny and the rice has started to brown underneath. Divide the rice and eggs among two plates. Flake the salmon over the top and scatter with the sesame seeds. Drizzle with dressing to serve.

Cambodian Seafood Amok SERVES **2** READY IN **15 MINUTES**

FOR THE RICE NOODLES
3½ ounces medium rice noodles
1 tablespoon peanut oil

FOR THE AMOK CURRY PASTE
½-inch piece fresh gingerroot
2 lemongrass stalks
3 garlic cloves
½ teaspoon turmeric

2 dried red chilies
½ teaspoon freshly ground black
  pepper
½ teaspoon sugar
scant ¼ cup peanuts
2 tablespoons peanut oil

FOR THE SEAFOOD CURRY
1 cup coconut cream

1 tablespoon fish sauce
½ lime
2 haddock fillets (about
  5½ ounces each)
4 ounces prepared raw mixed
  seafood, such as mussels, jumbo
  shrimp and squid rings
1 small handful of cilantro leaves

COOK THE RICE NOODLES in boiling water 4 to 5 minutes, or until soft,
or following directions on the package. Drain in a strainer and drizzle with the
oil to prevent the noodles from sticking together. Cover and set aside.

MEANWHILE, TO MAKE THE CURRY PASTE, peel the ginger, then remove
the tough outer leaves from the lemongrass and cut off the ends of the stalks. Peel
the garlic. Put all the curry paste ingredients into a mini food processor, and blend
into a smooth paste, adding a little water if necessary.

HEAT A LARGE WOK over medium heat and add the curry paste. Stir-fry
30 seconds, or until fragrant. Pour in the coconut cream and fish sauce for the
seafood curry, squeeze in the juice of the lime and mix everything together really
well. Bring the amok sauce to a boil while you prepare the fish.

CHOP THE HADDOCK into bite-size pieces. Add them to the hot amok sauce
followed by the mixed seafood. Gently mix everything together, reduce the heat to
low and simmer gently 5 to 6 minutes, stirring occasionally, until the fish starts to
flake and the seafood is cooked through.

WHILE THE AMOK COOKS, roughly tear the cilantro. Serve the curry with the
rice noodles, scattered with the cilantro.

Crawfish, Pink Grapefruit & Glass Noodle Salad SERVES **2** READY IN **15 MINUTES**

FOR THE GLASS NOODLE SALAD
5 ounces vermicelli rice noodles
1 pink grapefruit
2 scallions
1 ounce pea shoots or 1 handful of watercress

5½ ounces cooked shelled crawfish tails
1 small handful of basil leaves
1 small handful of mint leaves
2 tablespoons pumpkin seeds

FOR THE LEMONGRASS DRESSING
2 lemongrass stalks
2 limes
¼ teaspoon chili powder
2 teaspoons sugar
1 tablespoon olive oil

PUT THE NOODLES into a heatproof bowl and cover with boiling water. Cover the bowl and set aside 2 to 3 minutes to soften. Once soft, drain in a strainer and rinse with cold water. Drain again and squeeze out any excess water with your hands so that the noodles are really dry. Set aside.

MAKE THE DRESSING while the noodles soften. Remove the tough outer leaves from the lemongrass and cut off the ends of the stalks. Starting at the fatter end, roughly slice each lemongrass stalk into rings. You should see a purple band in the rings. Stop slicing when there are no more purple bands, then discard the rest of the lemongrass, because it will be too tough to eat.

GIVE THE LEMONGRASS SLICES a quick blast in a mini food processor until they are very finely chopped, then add them to a large mixing bowl. Squeeze the juice of the limes into the bowl with the lemongrass and add the chili powder, sugar and oil. Beat everything together to get the flavors going.

USING A SHARP KNIFE, cut the top and bottom off of the grapefruit, then stand it up on your cutting board. Carefully slice the skin off in sections, cutting from top to bottom. Remove any remaining pith, then cut the juicy pieces of grapefruit away from the membrane and put them into the bowl with the dressing. Squeeze in the juices remaining in the membrane. Trim and finely slice the scallions, then add them to the bowl. Add the pea shoots, crawfish, basil, mint and cooked noodles. Toss everything together well. Scatter the salad with the pumpkin seeds to serve.

Warm East-Med Eggplant & Tomato Salad SERVES 2 READY IN 15 MINUTES

5 tablespoons olive oil
2 teaspoons dried mint
2 eggplants
½ red onion
1½ lemons
½ red chili
heaped ⅔ cup cherry tomatoes

scant ⅔ cup pitted black olives
2 large handfuls of parsley leaves
½ teaspoon sumac
1 teaspoon ground cumin
2 tablespoons pine nuts (optional)
sea salt and freshly ground black
  pepper

PREHEAT THE BROILER to high. Meanwhile, put 3 tablespoons of the oil, 1½ teaspoons of the mint and a good pinch of salt in a mixing bowl, and stir well. Slice the eggplants into ¼-inch rings and brush both sides with the seasoned oil. Put the slices onto a broiler rack and broil 5 to 6 minutes, or until golden on one side.

WHILE THE EGGPLANT BROILS, peel and finely slice the onion and add it to a large mixing bowl. Squeeze in the juice of the lemons, add a pinch of salt and stir well. Finely chop the chili and halve the cherry tomatoes and stir them into the onion slices.

WHEN THE EGGPLANT HAS COOKED on one side, turn it over and broil another 5 to 6 minutes, or until golden on the other side and tender in the center.

TEAR THE OLIVES and rip the parsley leaves into the mixing bowl with the salad. Add the remaining oil and mint, and the sumac, cumin and a good pinch of black pepper. Toss everything together. Put the cooked eggplant slices into the bowl with the salad and gently stir everything together to combine. Serve the salad scattered with the pine nuts (if using).

Heather's Moroccan Paprika & Garlic Lentils SERVES **2** READY IN **20 MINUTES**

I stayed with Heather in her beautiful home just outside Marrakesh for a few days of sunshine and cooking. She taught me how to make many amazing dishes, including the classic cold Moroccan lentil salad. It was delicious, and I loved it hot straight out of the pan. She used a beautiful expression to describe when the dish was ready: "When the lentils have 'drunk all the water' it's done." Although my version is a little different, when the lentils have "drunk all the water" and the sauce is beautifully thick, you can add the lemon and herbs and then tuck in.

1 onion
4 garlic cloves
2 tablespoons olive oil
2 bay leaves
2 × 14-ounce cans green lentils
3 tablespoons tomato paste
1¼ teaspoons paprika

2 teaspoons ground cumin
1½ teaspoons freshly ground black pepper
1 teaspoon sugar
1 large handful of parsley leaves
½ lemon
sea salt

TO SERVE
extra virgin olive oil

PEEL AND FINELY CHOP the onion and garlic, then put them in a large saucepan, along with the olive oil and bay leaves. Cook over medium heat 5 to 6 minutes, stirring occasionally, until soft.

MEANWHILE, DRAIN AND RINSE the lentils, and set aside. Once the onion is soft, add the tomato paste, paprika, cumin, black pepper, sugar, lentils and a good pinch of salt. Pour in a generous 1¼ cups hot water and stir well. Bring to a boil and cook 5 to 6 minutes, stirring frequently, until the lentils have warmed through and the sauce is really thick.

WHILE THE LENTILS COOK, finely chop the parsley and add it to the pan with the lentils. Squeeze in the juice of the lemon and stir well, then drizzle with your fanciest extra virgin olive oil to serve.

Indian Cauliflower Soup SERVES 2 READY IN 15 MINUTES

This is such an awesome soup. It's rich, thick and packed with flavor. The ground spices provide a background layer of warmth, but it's the "temper" that really packs a punch. Tempering a dish means simply frying some spices in hot oil and pouring them into the dish at the end of cooking. It adds an extra layer of flavor, and it really brings the food to life.

FOR THE SOUP
1 small cauliflower
¾ cup vegetable stock
1¾ cups coconut milk
2 teaspoons garam masala
½ teaspoon turmeric
¼ teaspoon chili powder

14-ounce can lima beans
½ lime
sea salt

FOR THE TEMPER
1 onion
2 garlic cloves

2 tablespoons peanut oil
2 large pinches of dried
  curry leaves

USING YOUR HANDS, break up the cauliflower into very small florets and place them straight into a saucepan. Cover with boiling water and cook over high heat 6 to 8 minutes, or until tender.

MEANWHILE, POUR THE STOCK and coconut milk into a saucepan, and add the garam masala, turmeric, chili powder and a good pinch of salt. Stir well and bring to a boil over high heat. Reduce the heat to low and simmer gently. While the soup simmers, peel and finely chop the onion and garlic for the temper. Drain the lima beans in a colander and rinse with cold water.

ONCE THE CAULIFLOWER IS TENDER, drain, using the colander containing the beans. Add both to the saucepan with the soup. Remove from the heat and blend until smooth, using an immersion hand blender or adding it to a food processor. Return the soup to low heat and simmer gently, stirring occasionally, while you make the temper.

TO MAKE THE TEMPER, heat the oil in a skillet over high heat and add the onion and garlic. Stir-fry 2 to 3 minutes, or until golden. Remove from the heat. Rub the curry leaves between your hands to break them up and drop directly into the skillet. Pour the temper into the soup and squeeze in the juice of the lime. Stir well and serve.

Nice & Easy

In this chapter all the recipes are based on a really chilled-out approach to cooking for friends and family. I am talking about great food that is, quite simply, nice and easy to make. You can prepare any of these recipes armed with a glass of wine and not miss out on any of the fun, because they are all ready in 45 minutes or less. My Sumac Chicken with Black Gremolata & Tomato Salad is effortless and ready in 45 minutes. Amish's Gujarati Vegetable Curry, enriched with cashews and served with rice and chickpeas, is utterly sublime and takes only 35 minutes to make. Or my Mexican Sea Bream with Roasted Lemon Zucchini & Spicy Lime Seasoning has all the flavors to blow you away, but it only takes a cool 40 minutes to cook from start to finish.

Korean Braised Chicken with Rice Noodles SERVES **4** READY IN **35 MINUTES**

All Korean food should have a balance of five colors—black, white, yellow, green and red. Here, the black is from the soy, the white from the chicken, yellow from the noodles, green from the cilantro and red from the chilies.

1¼ pounds boneless, skinless chicken thighs
generous ¼ cup soy sauce
1 tablespoon oyster sauce
3 tablespoons rice wine or dry white wine
½ tablespoon sesame oil
2 tablespoons brown sugar

½ teaspoon ground ginger
½ teaspoon freshly ground black pepper
2 dried red chilies
4 garlic cloves
1 onion
1 carrot
1 zucchini

7 ounces vermicelli rice noodles
scant ½ cup chicken stock
2 scallions
½ red chili
1 small handful of cilantro leaves

ADD THE CHICKEN to a large, shallow flameproof casserole dish and pour in the soy sauce, oyster sauce, rice wine, sesame oil, brown sugar, ground ginger and black pepper. Crack open the dried chilies and add them to the dish, then peel and crush in the garlic. Stir everything together really well and place over medium heat.

PEEL AND ROUGHLY SLICE the onion, then peel the carrot. Chop the carrot and zucchini into matchsticks. Put the vegetables in the casserole dish with the chicken and stir to combine. It will look a little dry at this stage, but don't worry—the chicken and vegetables will produce lots of lovely juices. Bring to a boil, cover and reduce the heat to low. Simmer gently 15 minutes, or until the chicken is just cooked through.

MEANWHILE, PUT THE NOODLES in a large mixing bowl, cover with boiling water and let stand about 10 minutes to soften. Pour the stock into a small saucepan and heat gently over medium-low heat. Once the chicken is cooked, drain the noodles in a strainer and add them to the casserole dish in four little piles. Pour in the stock, then cover and cook another 10 minutes to allow the noodles to soak up the sauce. Trim and finely slice the scallions and red chili, then roughly tear the cilantro. Scatter the dish with the scallions, chili and cilantro to serve.

Roast Spatchcocked Chicken with Chimichurri & Rice & Black Bean Salad SERVES 4 READY IN 45 MINUTES

FOR THE CHICKEN
1 chicken (about
    3 pounds 2 ounces)
1 tablespoon olive oil
sea salt and freshly ground black
    pepper

**FOR THE RICE AND BLACK
    BEAN SALAD**
1 cup brown rice
1 cup canned black beans
½ red onion

1 large handful of mint leaves
1 large handful of parsley leaves
2 tablespoons sherry vinegar
⅔ cup cashews

FOR THE CHIMICHURRI
1 red chili
½ red onion
2 garlic cloves
1 large handful of parsley leaves
1 tomato
2 teaspoons dried oregano

2 teaspoons ground cumin
1 teaspoon smoked paprika
¼ cup olive oil
¼ cup sherry vinegar

FOR THE LEAF SALAD
4¼ ounces mixed salad leaves
½ lemon
1 tablespoon olive oil

PREHEAT THE OVEN to 425°F. Put the chicken onto a cutting board breast-side down. Using a pair of poultry shears, cut along either side of the spine from the neck to the rear cavity and remove it. Pull the two sides apart so that the chicken starts to open out, turn it over, breast-side up, and press down hard on each side so that the chicken flattens out. This will allow it to roast quickly and evenly.

LAY THE SPATCHCOCKED CHICKEN on a rack in a roasting pan and rub it all over with the oil. Season with salt and pepper. Roast 35 minutes, or until the chicken is cooked through and the juices run clear when the thickest part of the thigh is pierced with the tip of a sharp knife.

MEANWHILE, COOK THE RICE for the rice and black bean salad in boiling water 20 to 25 minutes, or until soft, or following directions on the package.

TO MAKE THE CHIMICHURRI, cut the top off the chili and roll the chili between your hands to remove the seeds. Peel the onion and garlic. Put all the ingredients for the chimichurri into a food processor or blender with a scant ½ cup water and a little salt, and blend to a coarse paste. Pour into a serving bowl, then cover with plastic wrap and set aside to allow the flavors to develop.

DRAIN AND RINSE THE BEANS for the rice and black bean salad, and add to a large serving bowl. Peel the red onion, then add it to a blender or mini food processor, followed by the mint and parsley. Process until finely chopped, then add to the bowl with the beans. Spoon in one-third of the chimichurri, add the sherry vinegar, season with salt and stir to combine.

HEAT A SMALL SKILLET over medium heat and add the cashews. Toast them 5 to 6 minutes, or until lightly golden, shaking the pan frequently to stop them from burning. Remove from the heat and set aside to cool.

PLACE THE SALAD LEAVES in a plastic food bag. Squeeze the juice of the lemon into the bag and add the oil. Seal the bag securely and shake it well until the salad leaves are coated in dressing. Pour the contents of the bag into a serving bowl.

PUT THE ROASTED CHICKEN onto a carving board. Drain the rice in a strainer and immediately refresh under cold water. Drain well and shake the strainer to remove as much water as possible. Add the rice to the bowl with the beans. Add the cashews and toss everything together until the grains of rice are completely coated with dressing. Serve slices of the lovely hot chicken with the rice and bean salad, the leafy salad and the chimichurri.

Sumac Chicken with Black Gremolata & Tomato Salad SERVES 4 READY IN **45 MINUTES**

FOR THE SUMAC CHICKEN
3 tablespoons olive oil
3¼ pounds chicken thighs
   and drumsticks on the bone
1 pound 2 ounces small new
   potatoes
1 red onion
1 garlic bulb
1 tablespoon sumac
2 teaspoons dried thyme
sea salt and freshly ground
   black pepper

FOR THE BLACK GREMOLATA
⅔ cup pitted black olives
1 dried red chili
¼ teaspoon sumac
1 large handful of parsley leaves
1 large handful of dill
3 tablespoons olive oil
2 teaspoons best sticky sweet
   balsamic vinegar
½ lemon
scant ½ cup walnut pieces

FOR THE TOMATO SALAD
10½ ounces mixed tomatoes,
   such as cherry, vine, baby, plum
2 tablespoons best sticky sweet
   balsamic vinegar
2 tablespoons olive oil
a pinch of sugar

PREHEAT THE OVEN to 400°F. Rub a little of the oil all over the bottom of a roasting pan and add the chicken pieces and new potatoes. Peel the onion, cut it into quarters and add it to the roasting pan. Break open the garlic bulb and remove 1 clove for the black gremolata, then scatter the rest of the cloves into the pan.

SEASON THE CHICKEN with the sumac and thyme, and a good pinch of salt and pepper. Drizzle everything with the remaining oil and mix all the ingredients in the pan together really well. Roast 35 to 40 minutes, or until all the chicken pieces are cooked through and tender, and everything is golden brown.

MEANWHILE, TO MAKE THE GREMOLATA, peel the reserved garlic clove, then add it to a mini food processor or blender, followed by the olives, chili, sumac, parsley, dill, oil, balsamic vinegar and a pinch of salt and pepper. Squeeze in the juice of the lemon and grind to a coarse paste. Add to a serving bowl and stir in the walnut pieces. Cover and set aside to allow those fantastic flavors to intensify.

TO MAKE THE SALAD, cut the tomatoes into different shapes and sizes, and put them in a serving bowl. Pour in the vinegar and olive oil, then season with the sugar, salt and pepper. Toss together gently, cover and set aside to allow the tomatoes to soak up the seasonings. Serve the chicken with the potatoes, gremolata and the salad.

Five-Spice Pork Belly SERVES **4** READY IN **40 MINUTES**

Mustard is the classic accompaniment to crispy pork belly in Hong Kong—
it works well and cuts through the richness of the meat. Get your butcher
or supermarket meat-counter assistant to score the fat of the pork belly to
help save you loads of preparation time.

FOR THE FIVE-SPICE PORK
2¾-pound piece of pork belly,
  skin scored
4 teaspoons Chinese five-spice
  powder
1 teaspoon ground Szechuan
  pepper
sea salt

FOR THE DIPPING SAUCE
3 tablespoons soy sauce
1 tablespoon rice wine vinegar
2 tablespoons honey
¼ teaspoon chili powder
1 garlic clove

FOR THE RICE AND BOK CHOY
1¼ cups jasmine rice
7 ounces bok choy

TO SERVE
scant ⅓ cup French mustard

PREHEAT THE OVEN to 500°F. Cut the pork belly into 2 pieces to help it cook
more quickly, and put both pieces, skin-side up, in a roasting pan. Rub the skin with
the Chinese five-spice powder, ground Szechuan pepper and a good pinch of salt. Put it
into the oven, reduce the heat to 425°F and cook 30 to 35 minutes, or until the pork is
cooked through and the skin is really crisp.

MEANWHILE, MAKE THE DIPPING SAUCE. Pour the soy sauce into a serving
bowl and add 2 tablespoons water, the rice wine vinegar and honey. Add the chili
powder, then peel and crush in the garlic. Whisk together, then cover and let stand to
allow the flavors to develop.

COOK THE RICE in boiling water 10 to 12 minutes, or until soft, or following
directions on the package, then drain in a strainer. Add boiling water to the saucepan
to a depth of 1 inch and place over low heat. Put the strainer with the rice over the pan,
cover loosely with a lid and let steam gently until you are ready to eat.

WHEN THE PORK HAS COOKED 25 minutes, cut the bok choy into quarters,
then put it into a steamer and steam over high heat 5 minutes, or until just tender.
Divide the sticky rice into four serving bowls and add the mustard to a serving dish.
Carve the pork and serve with the rice, bok choy, dipping sauce and mustard.

Thai Pork with Noodles & Lemongrass & Lime Dipping Sauce SERVES 4 READY IN 40 MINUTES

FOR THE ROAST PORK
1 pork loin (about
 1¼ pounds in weight)
4 garlic cloves
1 teaspoon freshly ground black
 pepper
½ teaspoon sugar
1 tablespoon rice wine
2 teaspoons fish sauce
1 tablespoon peanut oil

**FOR THE LEMONGRASS AND
 LIME DIPPING SAUCE**
2 lemongrass stalks
½-inch piece fresh gingerroot
1 handful of cilantro leaves and
 stalks
½ teaspoon chili powder
2 teaspoons sugar
1 tablespoon fish sauce
1½ limes

FOR THE NOODLES
5½ ounces green beans
7 ounces medium egg noodles
2 tablespoons peanut oil
1 tablespoon fish sauce
½ lime

PREHEAT THE OVEN to 400°F. Trim the pork and cut it into 4-inch pieces and pierce all over with a fork. Put the pieces of pork into an ovenproof dish, then peel and crush in the garlic. Add the black pepper, sugar, rice wine, fish sauce and oil. Mix everything together well and roast 30 to 35 minutes, or until the pork is just cooked through and tender.

MEANWHILE, TO MAKE THE DIPPING SAUCE, remove the tough outer leaves from the lemongrass and cut off the ends of the stalks. Peel the ginger. Put the lemongrass and ginger into a mini food processor, and add the cilantro leaves and stalks, chili powder, sugar and fish sauce. Squeeze in the juice of the limes and add ¼ cup water. Blend to a smooth sauce and pour into a serving bowl. Cover and set aside to allow all the amazing savory flavors to come together.

CUT THE BEANS for the noodles in half. Cook with the noodles in boiling water 4 to 5 minutes, or until the noodles are soft, or following the directions on the package. Drain and return to the saucepan. Pour in the oil and fish sauce, then squeeze in the juice of the lime. Stir well, cover and set aside until the pork is ready. Carve the pork into thick slices and serve it on a bed of noodles and beans with the dipping sauce on the side.

Rana's Keema Shepherd's Pie SERVES **4**   READY IN **45 MINUTES**

**FOR THE SPICY MASHED
  POTATOES**
1 pound 10 ounces new potatoes
2 tablespoons butter
1 teaspoon garam masala
3 scallions
1 tablespoon olive oil

FOR THE LAMB
1 red onion
2 tablespoons peanut oil
3 cardamom pods
3 large blades of mace
1 pound 2 ounces ground lamb
1 handful of cilantro leaves

FOR THE TOMATO SAUCE
1-inch piece fresh gingerroot
4 garlic cloves
heaped ⅓ cup tomato paste
1½ teaspoons garam masala
1 teaspoon chili powder
½ teaspoon ground cinnamon
scant 1 cup frozen peas
sea salt

COOK THE UNPEELED POTATOES in a large pan of boiling water 15 minutes, or until tender. Meanwhile, prepare the lamb. Peel and finely chop the red onion. Heat the peanut oil in a large skillet over medium heat and add the onion, cardamom pods and mace. Stir well, then add the lamb. Increase the heat to high and stir-fry 3 to 4 minutes, or until the lamb is just cooked through. Reduce the heat to medium and cook a few minutes, stirring occasionally, while you make the sauce.

TO MAKE THE SAUCE, peel the ginger and garlic, then add both to a mini food processor or blender, followed by the tomato paste, garam masala, chili powder, cinnamon and a good pinch of salt. Blend until smooth. Scoop the sauce into the pan with the lamb and add a scant ⅔ cup hot water and the peas. Stir well, cover, then reduce the heat to low and simmer gently 15 minutes, stirring occasionally.

DRAIN THE COOKED POTATOES, then return them to the pan. Mash lightly, so that they start to break up, then add the butter, garam masala and a good pinch of salt. Put the lid on the saucepan. Trim and finely chop the scallions, then add them to the pan and mix everything together well. Cover and set aside.

PREHEAT THE BROILER to high and finely chop the cilantro for the lamb. When the ground lamb is thick and rich, scatter with the cilantro and stir. Carefully pour the lamb mixture into an ovenproof dish and spoon the spiced potatoes evenly on top. Drizzle with olive oil and broil 5 minutes, or until crisp and golden and serve.

Lamb with Tarator Sauce, Mashed Potatoes & Tomato & Radish Salad SERVES 4 READY IN 40 MINUTES

Tarator sauce is a bread sauce with attitude and, served with lamb, is a classic Middle Eastern combination. It's packed with lemon juice, garlic, pine nuts, cumin and olive oil and it works beautifully with sweet and juicy lamb chops, gently flavored with allspice and oregano. The rich flavors of the lamb and sauce benefit from the contrasting fresh and simple tomato and radish salad, which was inspired by countless trips to the Eastern Mediterranean.

You may be thinking that mashed potatoes don't exactly sound like an exotic accompaniment for such a traditional, spiced dish—and they aren't. It is, however, my dad's favorite starch and, I agree, sometimes it's the only thing in the world that will do. In this case, the delicious simple mashed potatoes provide a bland creaminess that is the perfect vehicle to soak up all the yummy juices, so that nothing is wasted, and it goes surprisingly well with the spiciness of the roasted chops.

FOR THE MASHED POTATOES
1 pound 10 ounces new potatoes
3 tablespoons butter
sea salt and freshly ground black
  pepper

FOR THE TARATOR SAUCE
1 slice of white bread
1 garlic clove
1 lemon
heaped ⅓ cup pine nuts

1½ teaspoons ground cumin
scant ¼ cup olive oil

FOR THE LAMB CHOPS
8 small lamb chops
  (about 3¼ ounces each)
2 teaspoons ground allspice
2 teaspoons dried oregano
1 tablespoon olive oil

**FOR THE TOMATO AND RADISH
  SALAD**
heaped 1¾ cups cherry tomatoes
7 ounces radishes
2 scallions
1 handful of mint leaves
1 handful of parsley leaves
1 lemon
2 tablespoons olive oil

PREHEAT THE OVEN to 400°F. To make the mashed potatoes, cook the unpeeled potatoes in a large saucepan of boiling water 15 minutes, or until tender. Drain, return them to the pan, then add the butter and a good pinch of salt and pepper. Mash together until fairly smooth, then cover and keep warm.

MEANWHILE, MAKE THE TARATOR SAUCE. Tear the bread into small pieces and put them into a food processor. Peel the garlic and add it to the food processor. Squeeze in the juice of the lemon and add the pine nuts, cumin and a good pinch of salt and pepper. Add 3 tablespoons water and the oil, then blend to a coarse sauce. Scoop the tarator sauce into a serving bowl, add a grinding of black pepper, if you like, then cover and set aside.

PLACE THE LAMB CHOPS on a cutting board and gently score both sides with a sharp knife. Put the lamb in a mixing bowl and add the allspice, oregano, oil and a good pinch of salt and pepper. Mix well so that the lamb is completely coated. Set the lamb on a rack in a roasting pan and roast 8 to 10 minutes, or until tender and juicy.

MAKE THE SALAD while the lamb cooks. Halve the cherry tomatoes and radishes and put them in a serving bowl. Trim and finely chop the scallions with the mint leaves, if large, and add them, with the parsley leaves, to the tomatoes. Squeeze in the juice of the lemon, then pour in the oil and season with a good pinch of salt and pepper. Toss together well to combine and set aside. Serve the cooked lamb and mashed potatoes with the salad and tarator sauce.

Four Brothers Beef Curry SERVES **4** READY IN **30 MINUTES**

1 pound 10 ounces new potatoes
3 lemongrass stalks
3 garlic cloves
1 red chili
2 tablespoons peanut oil
4 cardamom pods
2 star anise
2-inch stick cinnamon

4 cloves
1¾ cups coconut cream
2 tablespoons tomato paste
2 tablespoons fish sauce
1 teaspoon sugar
4 sirloin steaks (about
   4½ ounces each)
1 lime

CUT THE UNPEELED POTATOES in half, then cook them in a large saucepan of boiling water 10 to 12 minutes, or until tender. Drain in a colander and set aside.

MEANWHILE, **REMOVE THE TOUGH** outer leaves from the lemongrass and cut off the ends of the stalks. Peel the garlic and cut the top off the chili. Add the lemongrass, garlic and chili to a mini food processor, and blend to a paste.

HEAT THE OIL in a large, shallow saucepan over medium heat and add the cardamom, star anise, cinnamon and cloves. Stir-fry 30 seconds until fragrant, then pour in the spice paste and stir-fry 10 seconds until it also releases its fragrance. Add the coconut cream followed by the tomato paste, fish sauce and sugar. Stir everything together to combine and simmer gently.

SLICE THE STEAKS into strips 2 inches wide and add them to the pan with the sauce. Carefully add the potatoes and mix well. Bring to a boil, then cover, reduce the heat to low and simmer gently 5 minutes. Remove the lid and cook another 10 minutes, stirring occasionally, until the beef is just cooked through and the sauce is nice and thick.

WHILE THE STEAK COOKS, cut the lime into quarters. Serve the beef curry with the wedges of lime on the side.

SOUKS, SAND & BERBER BEEF STEW

Morocco is an enchanting country. I love all it has to offer, from the art and architecture to the people, dramatic landscapes and wonderful food. My research for *Mighty Spice Express* took me there for several weeks, which included eating my way around Fez, the fabulous coastal town of Essaouira and several trips to Marrakesh.

I spent a very happy day in the sunny capital wandering through the *medina*, avoiding the rugsellers and drinking lots of mint tea. I love a rooftop, and I found a good one with a picture-postcard view of the city sprawled beneath the mighty Atlas Mountains, which were dusted with snow and gleaming under the vivid blue sky.

As the sun went down, the city came to life. The dusty souks were lit up by a thousand lightbulbs, and hungry diners were lured out into the cool evening by the delicious smells that were cast into the air from the food stands of the infamous Jamaa el-Fna square.

The vendors of Jamaa el-Fna sold everything. It was advanced street-food eating. I made several laps around the stands and decided on a rich stew that was cooked in an earthenware pot called a *tangier*. The stew was simply made from meat, spices and butter, which had been left to cook for hours so that the flavor gods could work their magic and turn it into something sublime. All good things come to those who wait, but thankfully not in this book, because with a few clever changes I have recreated a rather special version of this sublime Berber beef stew that's ready in only 45 minutes. You must give it a try!

Berber Beef Stew SERVES 4   READY IN 45 MINUTES

1 red onion
4 garlic cloves
1 carrot
2 zucchini
2 tablespoons olive oil
1 pound 5 ounces beef tenderloin
  or fillet
2 tablespoons tomato paste

2 teaspoons ground cumin
2 teaspoons ground ginger
1 teaspoon paprika
1 teaspoon freshly ground black
  pepper
½ teaspoon ground cinnamon
1 teaspoon flour
1 tablespoon honey

heaped ¾ cup couscous
1 large handful of parsley leaves
1 preserved lemon
heaped ¾ cup yogurt
2 tablespoons harissa paste
2 tablespoons toasted sliced
  almonds
sea salt

PEEL AND FINELY CHOP the onion and garlic, then peel the carrot. Chop the carrot and zucchini into ½-inch half-moons. Add the oil to a large saucepan over high heat and add the carrots and zucchini. Cook 4 minutes, stirring frequently, to soften.

MEANWHILE, CUT THE BEEF into ¾–1¼-inch cubes and add to the cooked vegetables. Add the onion and garlic, and stir well. Reduce the heat to medium, add the tomato paste, cumin, ground ginger, paprika, black pepper, cinnamon, flour, honey and 1 cup boiling water. Stir well, bring to a boil, then cover and simmer 10 minutes, or until the beef is just cooked through.

WHILE THE BEEF COOKS, put the couscous in a large mixing bowl and add ¾ cup warm water. Cover with plastic wrap and let stand 10 minutes, or until ready to serve.

FINELY CHOP THE PARSLEY while the couscous absorbs the water. Remove the flesh from the preserved lemon, finely chop the skin and set it aside. Discard the flesh. Pour the yogurt into a serving bowl, then stir in the harissa, cover and set aside.

REMOVE THE LID from the cooked stew, turn the heat up to medium and cook another 5 minutes, stirring occasionally, to allow the sauce to become lovely and thick. Add the parsley and preserved lemon skin to the cooked stew, and stir well. Fluff up the couscous with a fork and divide among four serving bowls. Divide the stew among the four bowls, scatter with the almonds and serve with the harissa yogurt on the side.

Mexican Sea Bream with Roasted Lemon Zucchini & Spicy Lime Seasoning SERVES **4** READY IN **40 MINUTES**

This meal tastes awesome and is so quick to make. The beauty of the dish comes from the flavor of the sauce, which has a pronounced smoky edge. I have taken a tip from Mexican cooking and charred the onion, garlic and tomatoes before adding them to a blender with spices to make the sauce. This might sound a bit fussy, but it only takes a few extra minutes and it adds so much to the overall flavor—and the smokiness is exaggerated even more by using chipotle chilies. Cinnamon and paprika create a sweeter background note to the sauce, which works so well with the fish. The flavors marry together as the sauce gently cooks for a few minutes before the fish fillets are added.

The dish is completed with zucchini roasted until they become soft and melt into creaminess when you eat them, and the whole thing is fired up with a wicked little chili, lime and salt seasoning, served at the table.

FOR THE LEMON ZUCCHINI
1 pound 5 ounces zucchini
3 large thyme sprigs
2 tablespoons olive oil
½ lemon
sea salt and freshly ground black
   pepper

FOR THE SEA BREAM
   AND SAUCE
2 chipotle chilies
1 red onion
4 garlic cloves
4 tomatoes
1 teaspoon ground cinnamon
½ teaspoon paprika
1 teaspoon brown sugar
leaves from 1 large thyme sprig
4 sea bream fillets (about
   4½ ounces each)
1 handful of cilantro leaves
2 tablespoons best-quality extra
   virgin olive oil

FOR THE SPICY LIME
   SEASONING
2 limes
1 teaspoon crushed chili flakes
1 teaspoon sea salt

TO SERVE
4 large flour tortillas

PREHEAT THE OVEN to 400°F. To make the lemon zucchini, cut the zucchini into generous ½-inch chunks and put them in a roasting pan. Add the thyme, olive oil and a good pinch of salt and pepper. Squeeze in the juice of the lemon and stir everything together well. Roast the zucchini 30 to 35 minutes, or until tender and creamy.

MEANWHILE, SOAK THE CHIPOTLE CHILIES for the sea bream sauce in 2 tablespoons hot water and set aside. Heat a nonstick skillet over high heat. While the pan heats, peel the onion and cut it into quarters, then peel the garlic. Carefully put them into the hot pan and toast 2 minutes. Add the tomatoes and turn the garlic. Cook another 2 to 3 minutes, or until the tomatoes and onion are charred on the cooked side and the garlic is charred on both sides.

WHILE THE TOMATOES ARE CHARRING, grate the zest of the limes for the spicy seasoning into a serving bowl and add the chili flakes and salt. Stir and set aside.

TRANSFER THE CHARRED INGREDIENTS and the chipotle chilies with their soaking liquid to a blender or food processor, and add the cinnamon, paprika, brown sugar, thyme and a good pinch of salt. Squeeze in the juice of 1½ of the limes used for the seasoning and blend to a smooth sauce.

POUR THE SAUCE into a large, shallow saucepan and bring to a boil over medium heat. Cook 10 minutes, stirring occasionally, then add the fish fillets, skin-side down, to the hot sauce. Cover and cook 4 to 5 minutes, or until the fish is beautifully tender and flaky.

PINCH THE SPICY SEASONING mixture between your fingers to release all the flavors while the fish cooks. Cut the remaining lime half into 4 segments.

SCATTER THE COOKED FISH with the cilantro and then drizzle with the extra virgin olive oil. Serve the fish with the cooked zucchini, tortillas, lime segments and the spicy lime seasoning on the side.

Dongbai Roast Cod with Stir-Fried Spinach & Peanuts SERVES 4 READY IN 25 MINUTES

This meal is a nod to my time in Dongbai, China. Fish was always served as part of any meal, along with, frankly, everything—meat, shellfish, vegetables, soups, stews and dumplings. The tables groaned with food, and that's definitely one of my favorite sights. Preparing multiple dishes is hard work, so I have stripped things back for this simple but mouthwatering version.

The combination of chili flakes, sesame seeds and cumin seeds was my favorite discovery from this region of northern China. The three flavors work perfectly together. I grind one-half of the mixture to a powder and leave the rest whole to create a spicy coating with a crunchy texture for the fish. The spices are enhanced by the rich flavors of oyster sauce, soy sauce and honey, giving the coating a salty–sweet base. These are big flavors, and the cod loves them all.

The simple spinach and peanut stir-fry is slightly tart to complement the sticky roast cod. Traditionally, this would be made with Chinese black vinegar, but this is hard to find and I actually really like the flavor of the red wine vinegar and soy sauce used here instead.

FOR THE RICE
1¼ cups jasmine rice

FOR THE ROAST COD
2 teaspoons crushed chili flakes
2 tablespoons sesame seeds
2 teaspoons cumin seeds

6 tablespoons oyster sauce
2 tablespoons soy sauce
1 tablespoon honey
1½ tablespoons peanut oil
4 skinless cod fillets (about 6 ounces each)

FOR THE SPINACH AND PEANUTS
1 tablespoon chili oil
heaped ⅓ cup peanuts
14 ounces spinach
1 tablespoon light soy sauce
2 teaspoons red wine vinegar

PREHEAT THE OVEN to 400°F. Cook the rice in boiling water 10 to 12 minutes, or until soft, or following directions on the package, then drain in a strainer. Add boiling water to the saucepan to a depth of 1 inch and place on low heat. Put the strainer with the rice over the pan, partially cover and let steam gently until you are ready to eat.

MEANWHILE, PUT HALF THE CHILI FLAKES, sesame seeds and cumin seeds for the roast cod into a spice grinder and grind to a fine powder. Pour into a mixing bowl and add the oyster sauce, soy sauce, honey and 1 tablespoon of the oil, and stir well. Add the fish and mix well to coat completely.

ARRANGE THE FISH in a small roasting pan in a single layer and spoon the remaining marinade all over the fish. Scatter the fish with most of the remaining chili flakes, sesame seeds and cumin seeds, and drizzle with the remaining oil. Roast 12 to 15 minutes, or until the fish is cooked through, tender and flaky.

MAKE THE SPINACH AND PEANUTS while the fish cooks. Heat a wok over high heat and add the chili oil and peanuts. Stir-fry 1 minute, or until just turning golden. Add the spinach and continue to stir-fry 2 to 3 minutes, or until wilted. Drain off any excess liquid and return the wok to high heat. Pour in the soy sauce and red wine vinegar, and continue to stir-fry another minute. Scatter with the remaining chili flakes, sesame seeds and cumin seeds. Serve the fish with the sticky rice and the spinach. Remember to spoon all the lovely juices from the roasting pan onto the fish— they are too good to waste.

Shrimp & Herb Brewat
with Vermicelli Rice Noodles SERVES **4** READY IN **30 MINUTES**

FOR THE SHRIMP AND HERB BREWAT
1 red onion
4 garlic cloves
2 tablespoons olive oil
heaped 1⅓ cups cherry tomatoes
1 cup tomato passata
1 teaspoon honey
2 teaspoons ground cumin
1 teaspoon paprika
½ teaspoon chili powder

½ teaspoon freshly ground black pepper
½ lemon
scant ½ cup vegetable stock
1 large handful of cilantro leaves and stalks
1 pound 2 ounces raw shelled jumbo shrimp (with or without tails)

FOR THE RICE NOODLES
1 large handful of cilantro leaves
7 ounces vermicelli rice noodles
2 tablespoons olive oil
½ teaspoon ground cumin
¼ teaspoon chili powder
½ lemon
sea salt and freshly ground black pepper

PEEL AND FINELY CHOP the onion and garlic. Place the oil in a large saucepan over medium heat. Add the onion and garlic. Stir-fry 4 to 5 minutes, or until golden.

MEANWHILE, CUT THE CHERRY TOMATOES in half, then add them to the cooked onion. Add the passata, honey, cumin, paprika, chili powder, black pepper and a good pinch of salt. Squeeze in the juice of the lemon and add the stock. Stir everything together really well, then bring to a boil. Cover and reduce the heat to low. Cook 10 minutes, stirring occasionally, to allow the sauce to develop in flavor.

ROUGHLY CHOP THE CILANTRO for both the brewat and the noodles, but keep them in separate piles. When the sauce has cooked, turn the heat up to medium. Add the shrimp and the pile of chopped cilantro leaves and stalks. Cook 5 to 6 minutes, stirring occasionally, until the shrimp have cooked through and turned pink.

WHILE THE SHRIMP COOKS, cook the noodles in boiling water 2 to 3 minutes, or until soft, or following directions on the package. Drain and return the noodles to the pan. Add the oil, the chopped cilantro leaves, the cumin, chili powder and a good pinch of salt and pepper. Squeeze in the juice of the lemon and stir everything together well so that all the spices and dressing completely coat the yummy noodles. Serve with the cooked shrimp and herb brewat.

Rita's Tamarind & Coconut Shrimp Curry SERVES **4** READY IN **20 MINUTES**

This is a super-quick shrimp curry, which is hot, sweet and sour all at once. If you can't find tamarind, just squeeze in the juice of a lime. And chili powder and freshly ground black pepper are fine if you don't have the whole spices.

1¼ cups basmati rice
2 onions
2 tablespoons peanut oil
3 dried red chilies

10 peppercorns
1 teaspoon paprika
½ teaspoon turmeric
1¾ cups coconut milk
3 teaspoons tamarind paste

1 pound 2 ounces raw shelled
  jumbo shrimp (with or
  without tails)
1 handful of cilantro leaves
sea salt

COOK THE RICE in boiling water 10 to 12 minutes, or until soft, or following package directions. Drain in a strainer and return to the pan. Cover the pan with a clean dish towel and then the lid. Set aside so that the rice can fluff up ready to eat.

MEANWHILE, PEEL AND FINELY SLICE the onions. Heat the oil in a large saucepan over medium heat and add the onions. Cook 4 to 5 minutes, stirring occasionally, or until just turning golden.

WHILE THE ONIONS COOK, add the chilies and peppercorns to a spice grinder, and grind to a fine powder. Pour the ground spices into the pan with the cooked onions and add the paprika, turmeric and a good pinch of salt. Stir well.

POUR IN THE COCONUT MILK and add the tamarind paste. Stir everything together really well so that the sauce takes on a rich red color. Bring to a boil and add the shrimp. Give them a good stir in the hot sauce, then cover and cook 5 to 6 minutes, stirring occasionally, until the shrimp are cooked through and beautifully pink. Meanwhile, roughly chop the cilantro. Scatter the cooked curry with the chopped cilantro and serve with the rice.

Condesa Smoky Beans with Green Salsa SERVES **4** READY IN **30 MINUTES**

FOR THE RICE
1¼ cups long-grain rice

FOR THE SMOKY BEANS
1 chipotle chili
2 × 15-ounce cans pinto beans
1 red bell pepper
1 red onion
2 tablespoons olive oil

2 bay leaves
4 garlic cloves
1 teaspoon ground cinnamon
2 teaspoons ground cumin
14.5-ounce can diced tomatoes
1½ tablespoons honey
2 ounces Gruyère cheese
sea salt

FOR THE GREEN SALSA
1 avocado
3 scallions
1 green chili
2 large handfuls of cilantro
   leaves and stalks
2 tablespoons olive oil
1 lime

COOK THE RICE in boiling water 10 to 12 minutes, or until soft, or following directions on the package. Drain in a strainer, then cover the rice with a clean dish towel while still in the strainer and set aside. Meanwhile, cut the chipotle chili for the beans in half and put both halves in a small bowl. Cover with 2 to 3 tablespoons boiling water and let stand to soften a couple of minutes.

DRAIN AND RINSE THE BEANS and set aside. Seed the pepper and peel the onion, then finely chop both. Place the oil in a large saucepan over high heat and add the pepper and onion. Stir-fry 3 minutes to soften, then reduce the heat to medium and add the bay leaves. Peel and crush in the garlic, and stir well.

ADD THE CINNAMON, cumin, tomatoes, honey and beans to the onion mixture and season with salt. Pour in the chipotle chili and its water. Stir well, cover and cook 15 minutes, stirring occasionally, or until the beans are hot and the sauce is thick.

MAKE THE GREEN SALSA. Cut the avocado in half and remove the seed with a knife. Scoop out the flesh into a blender or food processor. Trim the scallions and discard the top of the chili, then add them to the blender with the cilantro, oil and some salt. Squeeze in the lime juice and blend to a coarse salsa. Add to a serving bowl. Grate the cheese and scatter it onto the rice and beans. Serve with the salsa on the side.

Amish's Gujarati Vegetable Curry SERVES **4** READY IN **35 MINUTES**

This magnificent curry can be made well in advance by making the sauce and cooking it without any of the vegetables. Cook the vegetables, then refresh them under cold water. When you want to eat, reheat the sauce and add the vegetables. Cook until the vegetables have warmed through to serve.

1¼ cups basmati rice
14-ounce can chickpeas
1 onion
2 tablespoons peanut oil
1 inch piece fresh gingerroot
6 garlic cloves
4 tomatoes

heaped ½ cup cashews
2 teaspoons ground coriander
1 teaspoon ground cumin
1 teaspoon garam masala
½ teaspoon chili powder
½ teaspoon turmeric
14 ounces new potatoes

3 carrots
1 small cauliflower
7 ounces green beans
1 handful of cilantro leaves
sea salt

COOK THE RICE in boiling water 10 to 12 minutes, or until soft, or following directions on the package. Drain and rinse the chickpeas in a strainer. In the same strainer, drain the rice then pour the rice and chickpeas back into the pan. Cover the pan with a clean dish towel and then the lid. Let stand so the rice can fluff up.

MEANWHILE, PEEL AND FINELY CHOP the onion. Place the oil in a large saucepan over medium heat and add the onion. Cook 4 to 5 minutes, stirring occasionally, until golden.

PEEL THE GINGER and garlic, then add both to a blender or food processor with the tomatoes, ⅓ cup of the cashews, the ground coriander, cumin, garam masala, chili powder, turmeric and a good pinch of salt. Blend until smooth. Pour this mixture over the cooked onion, stir well and bring to a boil. Cover, reduce the heat to low and simmer 20 minutes, stirring occasionally.

QUARTER THE POTATOES while the sauce cooks. Cook them in boiling water 8 minutes. Peel the carrots, then cut them, with the cauliflower, into small pieces. Cut the beans in half. Add the vegetables to the potatoes. Cook 5 to 6 minutes, or until tender, then drain. Roughly chop the cilantro and set aside. Stir the vegetables into the sauce. Scatter the curry with the cilantro and serve with the remaining cashews.

Beirut Ratatouille SERVES **4** READY IN **45 MINUTES**

1 red onion
4 garlic cloves
2 tablespoons olive oil
5½ ounces button mushrooms
2 red bell peppers
1 eggplant
1 zucchini
14-ounce can chickpeas
scant ¼ cup tomato paste
14.5-ounce can diced tomatoes
3 teaspoons ground cumin

2 teaspoons paprika
½ teaspoon chili powder
½ teaspoon freshly ground black
  pepper
1 large handful of parsley leaves
sea salt

TO SERVE
1 lemon
1 bag of mixed salad leaves

PEEL AND FINELY CHOP the onion and garlic. Place the oil in a large saucepan over medium heat, add the onion and garlic and stir well. Roughly slice the mushrooms, then add them to the pan with the onion. Stir everything together and cook 3 to 4 minutes, stirring occasionally, until the mushrooms have cooked down.

MEANWHILE, SEED THE PEPPERS, then, chop the peppers, eggplant and zucchini into ¾-inch cubes. Drain and rinse the chickpeas. Transfer the vegetables to the pan with the cooked mushrooms and add the chickpeas, tomato paste, canned tomatoes, cumin, paprika, chili powder, black pepper and a really good pinch of salt.

POUR IN 1⅓ cups boiling water and stir well. Increase the heat to high and bring to a boil. Partially cover to allow the excess steam to escape, then reduce the heat to medium and simmer 25 to 30 minutes, stirring occasionally, until the vegetables are cooked through but still have a little bite.

AS THE RATATOUILLE SIMMERS, finely chop the parsley and cut the lemon into wedges. Add the salad to a serving bowl. Just before serving, mix the chopped parsley into the ratatouille. Serve with the lemon wedges and the mixed salad.

SOMETHING SPECTACULAR

There are times when you want to pull out all the stops, get out the fancy tableware, polish the glasses you've been saving for the queen and cook something unbelievable. In this chapter the recipes use fabulous ingredients to create spectacular dinners that can all be made super-quick—and none in more than 45 minutes. My Beautiful Beef Mezze—roasted tenderloin of beef, coated in spices and served with a spinach *raita*, and a tangy red onion and herb salad—takes only 40 minutes to make. Or my delicious Kashmiri Lamb Cutlets, served with a vibrant Pineapple & Chili Salad & Mint & Lime Raita, are utterly mind-blowing and ready for the table in 30 minutes. My delicate Essaouira Monkfish Tagine, flavored with preserved lemon, cumin, paprika and garlic, takes only 30 minutes to make. So, even if you don't have much time you can still impress your guests with something spectacular.

Chicken with Mexican Chili-Chocolate Mole, Polenta & Fennel Salad SERVES **4** READY IN **45 MINUTES**

Mole is an exquisite Mexican sauce with a complex flavor. It requires lots of ingredients and time, but I have created an express version that has all the depth of flavor of a traditional *mole*, without the fuss. Bright yellow polenta is just right to soak up all the intense flavors and is reminiscent of the corn used in Mexican cooking. My fennel salad, with crunchy radishes and a tart dressing, adds vibrancy and balances the flavors of the dish.

FOR THE CHILI-CHOCOLATE MOLE

6 garlic cloves
heaped ⅓ cup peanuts
4 cloves
2 chipotle chilies
1 onion
3 tablespoons olive oil
14-ounce can diced tomatoes
1 teaspoon ground cinnamon
1½ teaspoons ground cumin
2 teaspoons dried oregano

2 teaspoons brown sugar
1 ounce semisweet or bittersweet chocolate (70–85% cocoa solids)

FOR THE FENNEL SALAD

3½ ounces radishes
2 fennel bulbs
½ lime
2 tablespoons olive oil
sea salt and freshly ground black pepper

FOR THE GRILLED CHICKEN

2 tablespoons olive oil
4 skinless chicken breasts
1 tablespoon sesame seeds

FOR THE POLENTA

1⅓ cups quick-cook polenta
1½ tablespoons butter

FIRST, MAKE THE MOLE. Place a large skillet over medium heat, then peel the garlic and add it to the skillet with the peanuts and cloves. Toast 4 to 5 minutes, shaking the skillet occasionally, until the peanuts have started turning golden. While they toast, put the chilies in a bowl and add 2 tablespoons boiling water to soften them. Peel the onion and cut it into quarters.

PUT THE TOASTED PEANUTS, cloves and garlic into a blender or food processor. Add the chilies and their soaking water followed by the onion, oil, tomatoes, cinnamon, cumin, oregano, brown sugar and a really good pinch of salt. Blend 2 minutes until the sauce becomes beautifully smooth. Pour the sauce into a saucepan over medium heat and bring to a boil. Cover, reduce the heat to low and simmer 20 minutes.

MEANWHILE, MAKE THE SALAD. Cut the radishes into quarters and put them in a serving bowl. Shave the fennel using a slicer or mandoline and add to the bowl with the radish. Squeeze in the juice of the lime, pour in the oil and season with salt and pepper. Toss everything together really well, then cover loosely with plastic wrap and set aside.

TO MAKE THE GRILLED CHICKEN, heat a grill pan until smoking. Meanwhile rub the olive oil all over the chicken breasts. Cook 10 to 12 minutes on each side until cooked through and tender. Remove the pan from the heat and set aside.

WHEN THE MOLE SAUCE HAS SIMMERED 20 minutes, break in the chocolate and stir it in well. Cook another 10 minutes, stirring occasionally, to allow the flavors to develop even more.

MAKE THE POLENTA while the sauce finishes cooking. Pour the polenta into a saucepan and whisk in 3½ cups boiling water. Cook over low heat 1 to 2 minutes, stirring continuously, until the water is absorbed and the polenta cooked. Stir in the butter and a good pinch of salt and pepper. Serve the polenta with the chicken, with some rich, velvety brown mole sauce poured on top. Scatter each serving with sesame seeds and serve with the salad.

Saffron Chicken Mansaf with Tahini Yogurt & Green Salad SERVES **4**   READY IN **40 MINUTES**

A *mansaf* is a Jordanian dish traditionally made with lamb and served on a huge platter. The lamb is cooked with a thick yogurt sauce and served on a bed of rice scattered with nuts and herbs. It's a dish meant for sharing, as is this fast interpretation.

My version is made with chicken thighs instead of lamb and is seriously spiced up with saffron, cinnamon, cardamom and a heavy grating of nutmeg. Instead of making a traditional yogurt sauce, I have included a speedy variation using yogurt blended with wonderfully rich tahini and a squeeze of fresh lemon juice. Although I have used parsley, pine nuts and almonds to serve with the *mansaf*, you could add other herbs and nuts instead. Go crazy—for a great *mansaf*, the more you throw on top the better! The only thing I would insist on is that you share your *mansaf* with friends and family over a really good bottle of wine.

FOR THE SAFFRON CHICKEN MANSAF
1¾ cups basmati rice
generous 2½ cups chicken stock
¼ teaspoon saffron threads
2 onions
3 tablespoons olive oil
6 cardamom pods
4 garlic cloves
2 teaspoons ground cinnamon

3 bay leaves
1 pound 2 ounces boneless, skinless chicken thighs
heaped ⅓ cup pine nuts
1 large handful of parsley leaves
½ nutmeg
scant ⅔ cup sliced almonds
sea salt and freshly ground black pepper

FOR THE TAHINI YOGURT
scant 1¼ cups yogurt
2 tablespoons tahini
½ lemon

TO SERVE
1 bag of green salad

PUT THE RICE in a bowl, cover with cold water and stir. Set aside a few minutes to soak and to release the starch. Add the stock to a saucepan. Bring to a boil over medium heat. Once boiled, add the saffron, stir well and remove from the heat.

MEANWHILE, PEEL AND SLICE THE ONIONS. Place the oil in a large, shallow saucepan over medium heat and add the onions. Stir well and cook 4 to 5 minutes, stirring occasionally, until golden.

CRUSH THE CARDAMOM PODS by pressing down on them with the flat side of a knife blade. Add them to the cooked onions. Peel and crush in the garlic, then add the cinnamon, bay leaves and a good pinch of salt. Drain the rice and add it to the pan. Stir well to coat the grains in the oil and spices. Pour in the saffron stock and stir gently. Put the chicken thighs on the top of the rice and poke them down with a spoon. Bring to a boil, cover, reduce the heat to low and cook 20 minutes, or until the chicken is cooked through and the rice is tender.

WHILE THE CHICKEN AND RICE COOK, put the pine nuts in a small skillet over medium heat and toast 4 to 5 minutes, shaking the pan occasionally, until golden. Remove from the heat and set aside.

TO MAKE THE TAHINI YOGURT, pour the yogurt into a serving bowl, add the tahini and a good pinch of salt. Squeeze in the juice of the lemon, stir well and add a grinding of pepper. Set aside.

FINELY CHOP THE PARSLEY and set it aside. Add the salad to a serving bowl. Once the saffron mansaf is cooked, grate the nutmeg onto it and add half the pine nuts, sliced almonds and parsley. Season with salt and pepper, and stir everything together well with a fork. Scatter with the remaining nuts and parsley, and serve with the yogurt and green salad on the side.

COOL CHILIES, TEQUILA & TOSTADAS

The beautiful city of Oaxaca, in southern Mexico, has a really cool arty vibe. Little galleries are scattered throughout the city and the whole place is painted a veritable array of different colors. Art, music, dance and food form the cornerstones of life in Oaxaca, a city that provided a fantastic backdrop for my quest to find the best *tostadas*. *Tostadas* are the crunchy backbone of Mexican food—a crispy corn tortilla base covered in delicious toppings. It makes the perfect on-the-go street food.

I went high end with beautifully grilled octopus *tostadas* served on a fancy slate board and ate shredded pork *tostadas* with avocado and chili from a food cart. I also hit on Mercado Benito Juárez, a huge indoor market that was filled with wonderful fresh produce and awesome street food. They had deep-fried grasshoppers covered in salt and chili (the Mexican equivalent of crunchy chili peanuts to have with cheeky *cerveza*), spicy broths flavored with cilantro and lime, black beans served with soft tortillas for dunking and absolutely gigantic *tostadas*. The *tostadas* were actually more like pizzas, having a crispy base slathered in refried beans and topped with the famous Oaxaca *queso* (cheese).

I have combined elements from all my favorite *tostadas* to create a really fancy street-food-inspired dinner: Duck Tostadas with Black Beans & Salsa. It's a thing of deliciousness and takes only 35 minutes to make. Oh yeah, and add a shot of gold tequila before you eat, and you have a party.

Duck Tostadas with Black Beans & Salsa SERVES **4**   READY IN **35 MINUTES**

FOR THE ROAST DUCK
4 duck breasts
   (about 5½ ounces each)
4 garlic cloves
2 teaspoons smoked paprika
½ teaspoon chili powder
2 tablespoons olive oil

FOR THE BLACK BEANS
15-ounce can black beans
2 tablespoons olive oil
1½ teaspoons ground cumin
½ lime
sea salt and freshly ground black
   pepper

FOR THE SALSA
1 red onion

heaped ¾ cup drained sun-dried
   tomatoes in oil
1 teaspoon smoked paprika
½ lime

TO SERVE
1 lettuce
2 large handfuls of cilantro leaves
4 large tortillas

PREHEAT THE OVEN to 400°F. Trim and score the skin of the duck breasts, and put them in a small roasting pan. Peel and crush in the garlic, and add the smoked paprika, chili powder, oil and a good pinch of salt. Stir well to coat the duck completely. Turn the duck skin-side up, then roast 25 to 30 minutes, or until golden on the outside and juicy and pink in the center.

MEANWHILE, DRAIN AND RINSE the beans and pour them into a saucepan over medium heat. Mash the beans, using a potato masher, until fairly smooth, then add a scant ¼ cup water, the olive oil and cumin. Squeeze in the juice of the lime, season with salt and pepper, and stir well. Bring to a boil, reduce the heat to low and cook 8 to 10 minutes, stirring occasionally, until warmed through and thick. Remove from the heat, cover and set aside.

TO MAKE THE SALSA, peel the onion and cut it into quarters, then add it to a food processor, followed by the sun-dried tomatoes, smoked paprika and a pinch of salt. Squeeze in the juice of the lime, blend until smooth, then pour into a serving bowl.

FINELY SLICE the lettuce and cilantro, and put them onto a serving plate. Put the tortillas on four serving plates and cover each one with the beans. Slice up the duck and place it on top of the beans. Serve scattered with the salad and topped with some salsa.

Paprika & Fennel Pork Chops with Lentils & Beet & Goat Cheese Salad SERVES 4   READY IN 30 MINUTES

All my favorite flavors are brought together in this meal—pork, paprika, fennel, garlic, chorizo, lentils, beets and goat cheese. Although there's a lot going on, these big flavors go together splendidly and cook super quickly. Fennel seeds and smoked paprika make an aromatic crust for pork chops that are broiled to perfection. Chorizo fried with garlic, plus my favorite sun-dried tomato paste, enrich the lentils. And, finally, a quick salad of arugula, goat cheese and beets adds color, lightness and a little crunch to the meal. All this in 30 minutes—now that really *is* something spectacular!

FOR THE SPICED PORK CHOPS
1 tablespoon fennel seeds
2 teaspoons smoked paprika
4 pork chops (about 7 ounces each)
2 tablespoons olive oil

FOR THE LENTILS
4-ounce piece of chorizo
2 garlic cloves
1 tablespoon olive oil
14-ounce can green lentils
2 tablespoons sun-dried tomato paste
1 handful of parsley leaves
sea salt and freshly ground black pepper

FOR THE BEET AND GOAT CHEESE SALAD
7 ounces cooked, peeled beets
½ orange
1 tablespoon olive oil
1 handful of arugula leaves
2 ounces soft goat cheese
¼ red chili

PREHEAT THE BROILER to high. Lightly crush the fennel seeds using a mortar and pestle or a spice grinder. Add them to a mixing bowl followed by the paprika and a good pinch of salt. Put the pork into a separate mixing bowl, pour in the olive oil and stir well to coat.

TRANSFER THE PORK to a broiler rack and rub the spice mix over the top of the chops to give them a fantastic spicy crust. Broil the chops 6 to 8 minutes on each side, or until golden and cooked through.

WHILE THE PORK BROILS, finely chop the chorizo for the lentils and peel and chop the garlic. Place the oil in a skillet over medium heat and add the chorizo and garlic. Cook 3 to 4 minutes, stirring occasionally, until the chorizo turns golden. Drain and rinse the lentils, then add them to the pan with the cooked chorizo. Add the sun-dried tomato paste and ½ cup boiling water. Season with a pinch of salt and pepper. Stir well, reduce the heat to low and simmer gently, stirring occasionally, while you make the salad.

ADD THE BEETS to a mixing bowl and cut into small pieces using a knife and fork (this helps you avoid getting pink hands and a pink cutting board). Squeeze in the juice of the orange, pour in the oil and add a pinch of salt and pepper. Stir well and pour out onto a serving platter. Scatter the arugula over the beets and crumble the goat cheese over the top. Seed and finely chop the chili, then scatter it all over the salad. Cover loosely with plastic wrap and set aside.

FINELY CHOP THE PARSLEY for the lentils and add it to the pan with the warmed lentils. Turn the heat up to high, stir well and cook 1 to 2 minutes, stirring continuously, until thick. Serve the pork chops, spice-side up, with the lentils and the salad at the table.

Lao Lap Eggplant & Pork SERVES **4** READY IN **30 MINUTES**

2 red chilies
6 garlic cloves
5 tablespoons peanut oil
2 eggplants
2 tablespoons fish sauce

3 tablespoons dark soy sauce
1¼ cups jasmine rice
2 lemongrass stalks
1 handful of dill
1 handful of cilantro leaves

1 handful of mint leaves
1 pound 2 ounces ground pork
1 lime
1 handful of bean sprouts

CUT THE TOP OFF 1 of the chilies, then slice the chili. Peel the garlic, then slice 3 of the garlic cloves. Place 3 tablespoons of the oil in a large skillet over medium–low heat and add the sliced chili and garlic. Stir well and cook, stirring occasionally, while you prepare the eggplant.

SLICE THE EGGPLANTS into ¼-inch disks and layer them in the skillet. Add 1 tablespoon of the fish sauce and 2 tablespoons water. Cover and cook 20 minutes, or until tender, shaking the pan occasionally and turning the eggplant disks halfway through cooking. Remove the lid and add 2 tablespoons of the soy sauce. Turn the heat up to medium and cook 4 to 5 minutes, shaking the pan occasionally, until the eggplant disks have taken on a little color.

MEANWHILE, COOK THE RICE in boiling water 10 to 12 minutes, or until soft, or following directions on the package. Drain in a strainer. While the rice cooks, remove the tough outer leaves from the lemongrass and cut off the ends of the stalks. Cut the top off the remaining chili. Put the lemongrass, chili and remaining garlic into a mini food processor. Blend to a rough paste. Finely chop half the herbs and set aside.

HEAT A WOK over high heat until smoking. Add the remaining oil and the pork. Stir-fry 2 minutes, then add the spice paste and stir-fry another 2 to 3 minutes, or until the pork is just cooked through. Add the remaining fish sauce and soy sauce. Squeeze in the juice of the lime and stir-fry 1 minute. Turn off the heat, add the chopped herbs, stir well and set aside. Put the cooked eggplant on a large serving plate, spoon the pork on top and scatter with the remaining herbs and the bean sprouts. Serve with the rice.

Kashmiri Lamb Cutlets with Pineapple & Chili Salad & Mint & Lime Raita SERVES **4**   READY IN **30 MINUTES**

These lamb cutlets are flavored with wonderfully mild and beautifully red Kashmiri chilies, with the added warmth of ginger, cloves and garlic. The final grating of creamed coconut onto the lamb adds a hint of richness as it melts through. The flavor of the Kashmiri chilies is unmistakable and makes biting into the charred lamb a joyous experience. With every meal I eat I like to have a balance of flavors and textures, and the lamb cries out for something fresh and juicy. My salad of pineapple, chili, tomatoes, olives, mint and lime freshens things up in a blast of color and flavor, and the whole dish is finished off nicely with a mint and lime *raita*.

FOR THE LAMB CUTLETS
4 dried Kashmiri chilies
8 cloves
10 black peppercorns
1-inch stick cinnamon
1 teaspoon sea salt
1 teaspoon sugar
1-inch piece fresh gingerroot
4 garlic cloves
2 tablespoons white wine vinegar
2 tablespoons olive oil
8 lamb cutlets
1 ounce creamed coconut

TO SERVE
4 flatbreads

FOR THE PINEAPPLE AND CHILI SALAD
1 red chili
½ pineapple
1 cup cherry tomatoes
1 carrot
heaped 1 cup bean sprouts
¼ cup pitted black olives
1 handful of mint leaves
1 lime
2 tablespoons olive oil
sea salt

FOR THE MINT AND LIME RAITA
1 cup yogurt
½ lime
1 handful of mint leaves
1 tablespoon olive oil
a pinch of chili powder

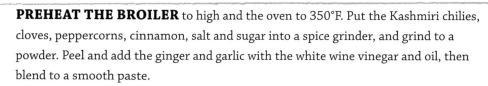

PREHEAT THE BROILER to high and the oven to 350°F. Put the Kashmiri chilies, cloves, peppercorns, cinnamon, salt and sugar into a spice grinder, and grind to a powder. Peel and add the ginger and garlic with the white wine vinegar and oil, then blend to a smooth paste.

PUT THE LAMB CUTLETS in a mixing bowl and add the spice paste. Stir well until the lamb is completely coated in the paste. Place the lamb on a broiler rack and broil 6 to 8 minutes on each side until golden on the outside and pink and juicy in the center.

WHILE THE LAMB BROILS, place the flatbreads in the hot oven and turn it off, so that they warm through and don't burn. Next, make the salad. Cut the top off the chili and roll the chili between your hands to remove the seeds, then chop it finely and add it to a large mixing bowl. Cut the top and bottom off the pineapple, then stand it upright on your cutting board. Slice off the skin, cutting downward from top to bottom. Carefully cut out any pieces of skin left on the fruit. Cut the pineapple half in half lengthwise, then slice off the woody core so that you are left with the soft flesh.

CHOP THE PINEAPPLE FLESH into small chunks and cut the cherry tomatoes in half. Add them to the bowl with the chili. Peel and then coarsely grate the carrot into the bowl, then add the bean sprouts and olives. Chop the mint leaves, if large, and add them to the bowl with the salad. Squeeze in the juice of the lime, pour in the oil and season with salt. Stir everything together to combine.

TO MAKE THE RAITA, pour the yogurt into a serving bowl, squeeze in the juice of the lime and season with a pinch of salt. Finely chop the mint and add it to the bowl. Stir well, drizzle with the oil and top with a pinch of chili powder. Grate the creamed coconut onto the cooked lamb to serve, with the vibrant salad, raita and warmed flatbreads on the side.

Manchurian Lamb with Tamarind Slaw & Grilled Chili Potatoes SERVES **4**   READY IN **40 MINUTES**

FOR THE ROAST LAMB
1 teaspoon Szechuan pepper
2 tablespoons sesame seeds
2 teaspoons cumin seeds
1¼ pounds trimmed neck or
   lamb loin fillet
2 tablespoons olive oil
sea salt

FOR THE GRILLED POTATOES
1 pound 2 ounces new potatoes
2 tablespoons chili oil

FOR THE TAMARIND SLAW
2 tablespoons tamarind paste
3 teaspoons honey
2 teaspoons soy sauce

2 teaspoons sesame oil
1 white cabbage (about 1 pound
   in weight)
4 scallions
½ red chili
1 handful of cilantro leaves

PREHEAT THE OVEN to 400°F. Add half the Szechuan pepper, sesame seeds and cumin seeds into a spice grinder and grind until smooth. Pour into a serving bowl and add the remaining spices and a good pinch of salt. Stir together well to combine.

IF USING LAMB LOIN, pull off the membrane. Cut the lamb into pieces 3 to 4 inches in size and add to a small roasting pan. Pour the olive oil over the lamb and mix well to coat. Scatter the lamb with two-thirds of the spice mixture and rub it all over meat. Roast 15 to 20 minutes, or until cooked through and really tender.

MEANWHILE, BOIL THE POTATOES 12 to 15 minutes, or until tender. While the lamb and potatoes cook, make the slaw. Combine the tamarind paste, honey, soy sauce, sesame oil and 2 tablespoons water in a large mixing bowl. Grate the cabbage using the fine setting of a food processor, then add to the bowl with the dressing. Trim and finely slice the scallions, then finely chop the chili and cilantro. Add them to the bowl with the cabbage and toss together thoroughly. Add to a serving bowl and cover.

HEAT A GRILL PAN over high heat. Meanwhile, drain the cooked potatoes and return them to the pan. Pour in the chili oil and add a pinch of the spice mixture and a small pinch of salt. Stir well, and don't be afraid to break up a few of the potatoes. Carefully pour the potatoes onto the hot grill pan and cook 2 minutes on each side, or until they start to crisp up, shaking the pan occasionally. Slice the lamb and sprinkle a little of the spice mixture on top. Serve with the potatoes and slaw, with the remaining spice mixture on the side.

Sticky Malaysian Lamb
with Penang Garden Rice SERVES **4** READY IN **40 MINUTES**

FOR THE STICKY LAMB
4 lamb rump steaks (about
   5½ ounces each)
1 teaspoon Chinese five-spice
   powder
2 tablespoons rice wine
2 tablespoons oyster sauce
1 tablespoon light soy sauce

1 teaspoon sesame oil
1 teaspoon olive oil

FOR THE PENANG RICE
1¾ cups basmati rice
1-inch piece fresh gingerroot
1 onion
2 lemongrass stalks

2 tablespoons peanut oil
1 teaspoon fenugreek seeds
1-inch stick cinnamon
4 cardamom pods
3 star anise
1¾ cups coconut milk
1 small handful of cilantro leaves
3 tablespoons fish sauce

PREHEAT THE OVEN to 400°F. Put the lamb in a small roasting pan and add the Chinese five-spice powder, rice wine, oyster sauce, soy sauce, sesame oil and olive oil. Stir well and set aside to marinate.

PUT THE RICE in a large saucepan, cover with cold water and stir. Let stand 5 minutes to soak.

PEEL THE GINGER and onion, then finely chop both. Bash the fat ends of the lemongrass with a wooden spoon. Place the peanut oil in a shallow saucepan over medium heat and add the fenugreek, cinnamon, cardamom and star anise. Stir-fry 30 seconds until fragrant, then add the onion and ginger. Cook 4 to 5 minutes, stirring occasionally, until the onion has started to turn golden.

MEANWHILE, PLACE THE LAMB in the oven 15 to 20 minutes, or until cooked through and tender.

POUR THE SOAKED RICE into a strainer, then add it to the pan with the cooked onion and spices. Pour in 1¾ cups hot water and the coconut milk. Add the lemongrass to the pan, then stir and cover. Reduce the heat to low and simmer gently 10 to 15 minutes, or until all the water has been absorbed and the rice is tender. You can always add extra hot water if the rice needs it. Slice the cooked lamb.

CHOP THE CILANTRO, then season the cooked rice with the fish sauce. Add to a serving dish. Place the lamb on top of the rice and scatter with cilantro leaves to serve.

Beautiful Beef Mezze SERVES 4 READY IN 40 MINUTES

I always enjoy a mezze—a table laden with wonderful homemade food to pass around to great friends and family, while the conversation and wine flow. I couldn't resist including a super-fast version in this book, and this beef mezze, inspired by the Eastern Mediterranean, has it all—spice-encrusted roast beef, a spinach *raita*, a crunchy salad and warm flatbreads.

Before roasting, the beef is smothered in a paste of spices, lemon and garlic, which penetrate the meat while it cooks. My vibrant salad of red onions and tomatoes, with loads of fresh cilantro and parsley, and doused in lime juice and olive oil, acts as a sidekick to the beef. My twist on a traditional *raita* uses spinach stir-fried with garlic and mixed into the cooling yogurt, topped with toasted pine nuts. It's a heavenly combination. Just make sure you squeeze all the excess moisture out of the cooked spinach first. My favorite way to eat this meal is to stuff a flatbread with beef and salad, drizzle over plenty of *raita*, roll it all up and go for it!

FOR THE ROAST BEEF
1¼-pound piece of beef tenderloin
4 garlic cloves
2 teaspoons paprika
2 teaspoons ground cumin
1 teaspoon ground coriander
2 tablespoons olive oil
1 lemon
sea salt and freshly ground black
  pepper

FOR THE SPINACH RAITA
2 garlic cloves
2 tablespoons olive oil
scant ¼ cup pine nuts
7 ounces baby spinach
scant 1 cup Greek yogurt
1 lemon

**FOR THE ONION, TOMATO AND
  HERB SALAD**
2 red onions
1½ limes
2 large tomatoes
2 large handfuls of cilantro leaves
2 large handfuls of parsley leaves
2 tablespoons olive oil

TO SERVE
4 flatbreads

PREHEAT THE OVEN to 400°F and take the beef out of the fridge to come to room temperature. Peel the garlic, then add it to a mini food processor, followed by the paprika, cumin and ground coriander. Add the olive oil and a good pinch of salt and pepper. Squeeze in the juice of the lemon and blend until smooth.

PUT THE BEEF IN A ROASTING PAN, then add the paste and rub it all over the beef. Roast 30 to 35 minutes, or until charred on the outside and beautifully tender on the inside.

WHILE THE BEEF COOKS, peel and slice the garlic for the raita. Heat the oil in a wok over high heat and add the pine nuts. Stir-fry 30 seconds, or until golden, then remove from the pan and set aside. Add the garlic to the pan. Stir-fry for 30 seconds, or until golden, then add the spinach and a pinch of salt. Stir-fry a further 2 to 3 minutes, or until the spinach has completely wilted. Add the spinach to a fine strainer to drain.

TO MAKE THE SALAD, peel and finely slice the red onions, then add them to a mixing bowl. Squeeze in the juice of the limes and add a good pinch of salt. Stir to combine and set aside.

USING THE BACK OF A SPOON, squeeze any excess moisture out of the spinach. Add to a serving bowl along with the yogurt, then squeeze in the juice of the lemon and season with salt and pepper. Stir well, scatter with the pine nuts, then cover.

CUT THE TOMATOES for the salad in half and squeeze out the seeds. Finely chop the flesh and put it into the bowl with the onions. Finely chop the herbs and add them to the bowl. Pour in the oil, add a pinch of pepper and stir well to combine.

PLACE THE FLATBREADS in the oven 2 minutes to warm through. When the beef is cooked, remove it from the oven and transfer it to a carving board. Slice the beef and serve it with the warm flatbreads, spinach raita and salad. Oh, and a glass or two of red.

Korean Steaks with Carrot Kimchi & Sanjim SERVES **4** READY IN **40 MINUTES**

FOR THE CARROT KIMCHI
2¼ pounds carrots
¼ cup salt
1-inch piece fresh gingerroot
1 garlic clove
1 tablespoon fish sauce
2 teaspoons sugar
1 teaspoon chili powder

3 tablespoons yogurt
½ teaspoon honey
2 handfuls of chives

FOR THE SANJIM
1 garlic clove
12 scallions
½ cup walnuts
1 tablespoon light soy sauce

2 tablespoons chili sauce
2 teaspoons honey
2 teaspoons sesame oil

FOR THE GRILLED STEAKS
2 tablespoons olive oil
4 rib-eye steaks (about
   9 ounces each)
sea salt and freshly ground black
   pepper

TO MAKE THE KIMCHI, peel the carrots then grate them using a food processor. Add them to a large mixing bowl along with the salt and 3¼ cups boiling water. Stir to combine with a wooden spoon and set aside 20 minutes. Meanwhile, make the dressing for the kimchi. Peel and grate the ginger into a serving bowl, then peel and crush in the garlic. Add the fish sauce, sugar, chili powder, yogurt and honey. Finely chop the chives and add them to the bowl. Stir well, then cover and set aside.

TO MAKE THE SANJIM, peel the garlic and trim the scallions, then add them both to a mini food processor, followed by the walnuts. Blend to a coarse mixture. Scoop into a serving bowl and add the soy sauce, chili sauce, honey and sesame oil. Stir well to combine, then cover and set aside.

TO COOK THE STEAKS, heat a grill pan over high heat until smoking. Rub the olive oil all over the steaks and season both sides with salt and pepper. Cook the steaks 2 to 3 minutes on each side until beautifully charred on the outside but still perfectly pink in the center. Remove from the heat and set aside to rest the meat.

DRAIN AND RINSE THE CARROTS thoroughly under cold water. Repeat several times to remove all the salt. Squeeze out any excess water using your hands and add the carrots to the bowl with the dressing. Stir well and serve with the steaks and sanjim.

Essaouira Monkfish Tagine SERVES **4** READY IN **30 MINUTES**

1¼-pound monkfish fillet, membrane removed
½ lemon
heaped ¾ cup couscous
2 carrots
4 garlic cloves
2 red bell peppers

3 tablespoons olive oil
2 teaspoons ground cumin
1 teaspoon paprika
½ teaspoon freshly ground black pepper
¼ teaspoon chili powder
1 teaspoon sugar

14.5-ounce can diced tomatoes
1 preserved lemon
¼ cup pitted black olives
1 large handful of parsley leaves
sea salt

CUT THE MONKFISH into 2 pieces and put them in a mixing bowl. Squeeze the juice of the lemon all over the fish, sprinkle with a pinch of salt and set aside. Add the couscous to a large mixing bowl and add ¾ cup warm water. Cover with plastic wrap and leave a minimum of 10 minutes, or until ready to serve.

PEEL THE CARROTS and garlic, and seed the peppers, then finely slice them all. Place the oil in a large saucepan over high heat and add the peppers and carrots. Cook 5 to 6 minutes, stirring occasionally, until they start to soften. Reduce the heat to medium and add the garlic, cumin, paprika, black pepper, chili powder, sugar and a pinch of salt, and stir well.

ADD THE TOMATOES, pour in a scant 1 cup hot water and stir well to combine. Bring to a boil and add the fish. Partially cover with a lid and cook 5–6 minutes. Turn the fish over, spoon some sauce on top of it, then cover with the lid and cook another 5 to 6 minutes, or until the fish is cooked through and tender.

WHILE THE FISH COOKS, remove and discard the flesh from the preserved lemon. Slice the skin into thin strips and set aside. Slice the olives and finely chop the parsley, then set aside. Fluff up the couscous with a fork. Stir the preserved lemon skin, olives and parsley into the pan with the cooked fish, and mix well. To serve, cut the pieces of fish in half and serve with the couscous.

Phuket Snapper with Hoisin Noodles & Herb Salad SERVES **4**   READY IN **40 MINUTES**

This delicious meal was inspired by our family vacation in Phuket a few years ago. I found hanging out and cooking with the superb chef, Jitty, at our villa way more interesting than spending a lazy afternoon by the pool. In her tiny, but immaculate, kitchen she would cook up a storm for every meal. She had trained in Bangkok and knew about the regional cuisines of Thailand. Her repertoire of dishes was incredible, and her use of flavor, color and texture was spot on. I have borrowed a few elements from her glorious kitchen and added my own express twist to them so that you can get a Thai feast on the table in only 40 minutes.

The Worcestershire sauce is the secret ingredient in this dish, as used in Thailand. (I would have gone for fish sauce!) Worcestershire sauce adds a wicked flavor that most people won't recognize. It's strange that a British ingredient works so well with Thai flavors, but this is exactly why I love cooking—you can mix and match to create something sublime.

FOR THE ROASTED SNAPPER
1 tablespoon peanut oil, plus extra
  for greasing
2 red snapper (about
  1 pound 2 ounces each), cleaned
2 lemongrass stalks
1 lime
2-inch piece fresh gingerroot
1 tablespoon Worcestershire sauce
1 teaspoon freshly ground black
  pepper
sea salt

FOR THE HERB SALAD
2 lemongrass stalks
1-inch piece fresh gingerroot
½ red chili
2 tablespoons fish sauce
1½ teaspoons sugar
1 red onion
1½ limes
10½ ounces carrots
2 large handfuls of cilantro leaves
2 large handfuls of basil leaves
1 large handful of mint leaves
scant ¼ cup peanuts

FOR THE HOISIN NOODLES
7 ounces medium egg noodles
3 tablespoons hoisin sauce
2 tablespoons soy sauce
1 tablespoon peanut oil

PREHEAT THE OVEN to 400°F. Oil a piece of foil large enough to wrap the fish in, and put the snapper on top. Finely slice the lemongrass, lime and unpeeled ginger.

SPOON THE WORCESTERSHIRE SAUCE into the cavity of the fish and stuff with the sliced lemongrass, lime and ginger, putting a few slices of lime on the top, if you like. Drizzle with the oil and season with black pepper and a good pinch of salt. Wrap the fish tightly in the foil and place in a roasting pan. Roast the fish 25 to 30 minutes, or until cooked through and tender.

MEANWHILE, MAKE THE SALAD. Remove the tough outer leaves of the lemongrass and cut off the ends of the stalks. Peel the ginger. Put the lemongrass into a mini food processor with the ginger, chili, fish sauce and sugar, then blend to a smooth paste. Peel, then grate the onion into a large mixing bowl and squeeze the juice of the limes onto the grated onion (this will help take the rawness out of the onions). Stir well to combine. Peel, then grate the carrots on top of the onions.

FINELY CHOP MOST OF THE HERBS, reserving a few leaves to garnish, and add to the bowl with the salad. Pour in the spice paste, toss everything together and transfer to a serving bowl. Cover and set aside.

COOK THE NOODLES in boiling water 4 to 5 minutes, or until soft, or following directions on the package. Drain the noodles and return them to the pan. Pour in the hoisin sauce, soy sauce and oil. Stir well to combine, then pour the noodles onto a serving dish and set aside. Scatter the salad with the peanuts and reserved herb leaves. Unwrap the cooked fish and set it on a large plate. Serve the fish at the table with the noodles and salad.

Keralan Seafood Curry SERVES **4** READY IN **25 MINUTES**

1¼ cups basmati rice
1-inch piece fresh gingerroot
6 garlic cloves
1 green chili
2 teaspoons ground coriander
½ teaspoon turmeric
heaped 1¾ cups cherry tomatoes

2 tablespoons peanut oil
2 teaspoons black mustard seeds
2 large pinches dried curry leaves
13.5-fluid-ounce can coconut milk
½ lime
9 ounces boneless tilapia fillets or
   other white fish fillets

¾ pound mixed seafood, such as
   squid rings, raw shelled jumbo
   shrimp, shelled mussels
1 handful of cilantro leaves
sea salt

COOK THE RICE in boiling water 10 to 12 minutes, or until soft, or following directions on the package. Drain in a strainer and return to the pan. Cover the pan with a clean dish towel and then the lid. Set aside to allow the rice to fluff up.

MEANWHILE, PEEL THE GINGER AND GARLIC, and cut the top off the chili, then put these ingredients into a mini food processor with the ground coriander, turmeric and a good pinch of salt. Blend to a smooth paste, adding a little water if necessary, and set aside.

CUT THE CHERRY TOMATOES in half and reserve. Place the oil in a large saucepan over medium heat and add the mustard seeds and curry leaves. Let them crackle a few seconds, then add the spice paste. Stir-fry 30 seconds, or until fragrant, then pour in the coconut milk. Squeeze in the juice of the lime and add a pinch of salt. Stir everything together well to combine and bring to a boil.

CHOP THE FISH into large, bite-size pieces and add to the boiling sauce, then add the seafood and cherry tomatoes and stir gently. Bring back to a boil, cover and reduce the heat to medium-low. Cook 6 to 8 minutes, stirring occasionally, until all the seafood is cooked through and tender. Scatter the cooked curry with the cilantro leaves and serve with the rice.

Iain's Mighty Scallop Ceviche with Buckwheat Noodles & Avocado Salad SERVES 4   READY IN 30 MINUTES

This is a super-fast, tangy and spicy dinner inspired by southeastern Asia, with a bit of good old West London in there as well. Iain is one of my best friends, and he cooks a mean scallop. Ceviche is simply raw fish, or certain types of shellfish, that has been "cooked" in an acid, such as lime juice or vinegar. Make sure you buy the freshest seafood you can on the day you want to serve the dish. If you want to reduce the chili heat, remove the seeds—and if you like it to be a bit more piquant, throw in an extra chili.

FOR THE SCALLOP CEVICHE

scant ¼ cup peanuts
2 lemongrass stalks
3 scallions
1 red chili
¾ pound scallops
2 limes
2 tablespoons fish sauce
1 teaspoon sugar
1 large handful of mint leaves

FOR THE BUCKWHEAT NOODLES

3 scallions
7 ounces buckwheat noodles
3 tablespoons soy sauce
2 tablespoons olive oil
1 teaspoon sesame oil

FOR THE AVOCADO SALAD

2 tablespoons red wine vinegar
2 teaspoons sugar
2 tablespoons olive oil
1 teaspoon sesame oil
1 teaspoon ground coriander
2 ripe avocados
1 tablespoon pumpkin seeds
sea salt

ROUGHLY CHOP THE PEANUTS and put them in a skillet over medium heat. Toast the peanuts 4 to 5 minutes, shaking the pan occasionally, until golden. Remove from the heat and set aside to cool.

MEANWHILE, REMOVE THE TOUGH outer leaves from the lemongrass and cut off the ends of the stalks. Trim all the scallions for the ceviche and the noodles. Cut the top off the chili, then finely chop half the chili with 3 scallions and the lemongrass, and put them into a bowl for the ceviche. Finely chop the remaining scallions and chili half, and put them in a separate small bowl to add to the noodles later.

COOK THE NOODLES in boiling water 5 to 7 minutes, or until soft, or following directions on the package. While the noodles cook, thinly slice the scallops horizontally and arrange them in an even layer in a shallow serving dish. Squeeze the juice of the limes all over the scallop slices and shake the dish so all the slices are coated. Cover with plastic wrap and set aside 8 to 10 minutes so the scallops can "cook" in the acid and turn slightly opaque in color. Remember to shake the dish from time to time.

WHEN THE NOODLES HAVE COOKED, drain them in a strainer, refresh under cold water and drain again. Return them to the pan and dress with the soy sauce, olive oil and sesame oil. Stir well to coat, then add the noodles to a serving bowl. Scatter with the reserved chopped chili and scallions. Cover loosely with plastic wrap and set aside.

MAKE THE DRESSING for the salad by whisking the red wine vinegar and sugar together in a mixing bowl until the sugar dissolves. Pour in the olive oil and sesame oil, then add the coriander and a pinch of salt. Whisk everything together well.

CUT THE AVOCADOS in half and remove the seeds with a knife. Scoop out small pieces of the flesh using a teaspoon and put them into the bowl with the dressing. Carefully mix everything together so that the avocado does not discolor. Arrange the avocado on a serving plate and scatter with the pumpkin seeds. Cover and set aside.

ADD THE FISH SAUCE to the "cooked" scallops, then add the sugar and the reserved chopped chili, scallions and lemongrass, and carefully toss together. Tear up the mint leaves and scatter them, along with the toasted peanuts, onto the scallops. Serve with the noodles and avocado salad.

Panjim Clams with Coconut Okra SERVES **4** READY IN **30 MINUTES**

FOR THE CLAMS
1 onion
1 green chili
2 tablespoons peanut oil
2 teaspoons garam masala
1 teaspoon turmeric
1¾ cups coconut cream
½ lime
2¼ pounds picked and
  cleaned clams

1 small handful of cilantro leaves
sea salt

FOR THE COCONUT OKRA
¾ pound okra
1 red onion
3 garlic cloves
1 green chili
2 cardamom pods
2 tablespoons peanut oil

8 black peppercorns
¾ cup coconut cream
1 large pinch of dried curry leaves
3 tablespoons raisins
½ lime

TO SERVE
4 small naan breads

PREHEAT THE OVEN to 350°F. Peel the onion and cut the top off the chili. Finely chop both. Place the oil in a saucepan over medium heat and add both ingredients. Stir-fry 4 to 5 minutes, or until just turning golden.

ADD THE GARAM MASALA and turmeric, stir well and pour in the coconut cream. Squeeze in the juice of the lime and add a good pinch of salt. Stir well, reduce the heat to low and simmer gently, stirring occasionally, while you start the okra.

CUT THE TOPS off the okra. Peel the red onion and garlic, and cut the top off the chili, then finely chop the onion, garlic and chili. Split the cardamom pods open by pressing down on them with the flat side of a knife blade. Add the oil to a wok over high heat and add the onion, garlic, chili, cardamom and peppercorns. Stir-fry 2 to 3 minutes, or until the garlic is just golden, then add the okra and a good pinch of salt. Stir-fry 2 minutes, then add the coconut cream. Add the curry leaves to the wok by rubbing them between your hands and letting them drop into the wok. Stir well to combine, cover and reduce the heat to low. Let cook 5 minutes.

MEANWHILE, PLACE THE NAAN in the oven and switch it off, so that they just warm through. Stir the raisins and the juice of the lime into the half-cooked okra, then cover and cook 5 minutes, or until the okra is tender. While the okra finishes cooking, add the clams to the hot sauce, cover and cook 4 to 5 minutes, shaking the pan occasionally, until the clams have opened. Discard any that remain closed. Chop the cilantro and scatter it onto the clams. Serve with the okra and warmed naan breads.

Rooftop-Roasted Vegetables with Chili Tapenade SERVES **4** READY IN **45 MINUTES**

**FOR THE ROOFTOP-
  ROASTED VEGETABLES**
2 red onions
2 red bell peppers
2 zucchini
1 eggplant
3 tablespoons olive oil
1 tablespoon dried thyme

heaped 1¾ cups cherry tomatoes
1 loaf of fabulously crusty bread
heaped ⅓ cup pine nuts
2 large handfuls of mint
½ lemon
3½ ounces feta cheese
sea salt and freshly ground black
  pepper

FOR THE CHILI TAPENADE
1 garlic clove
⅔ cup pitted black olives
4 anchovy fillets
1 large handful of parsley leaves
¼ teaspoon chili powder
1½ teaspoons ground cumin
2 tablespoons olive oil
½ lemon

PREHEAT THE OVEN to 400°F. Peel the onions and seed the peppers, then cut the onions, peppers, zucchini and eggplant into large bite-size pieces and put them in a roasting pan. Pour the olive oil evenly over the vegetables, then scatter with the thyme and a good pinch of salt and pepper. Stir everything together really well and roast 25 minutes, or until the vegetables are almost cooked through.

WHILE THE VEGETABLES ARE COOKING, make the chili tapenade. Peel the garlic and put it into a blender or food processor. Add the olives, anchovies, parsley, chili powder, cumin, oil and a pinch of salt and pepper. Squeeze in the juice of the lemon and blend to a coarse paste. Pour into a serving bowl, cover loosely with plastic wrap and let stand to allow the savory flavors to develop.

WHEN THE VEGETABLES have almost cooked, remove from the oven and scatter with the tomatoes. Cook another 8 to 10 minutes, or until all the vegetables are tender and golden and the tomatoes have just started to break down. Put the bread in the oven for the last 5 minutes to warm through.

PUT THE PINE NUTS into a small skillet over medium heat and toast 2 to 3 minutes, shaking the pan occasionally, until golden. Remove from the heat and set aside. Strip the mint leaves from the stems. Squeeze the juice of the lemon evenly over the cooked vegetables, then scatter with crumbled feta cheese, the mint leaves and the toasted pine nuts. Serve with the chili tapenade and warm bread.

Sesame Eggplant Curry with Keralan Spinach & Kernel Corn Salad SERVES **4** READY IN **45 MINUTES**

This vegetarian feast is my take on a classic northern Indian curry. It's served with a fresh spinach and kernel corn dish, hailing from Kerala, which is a cross between a side dish and a salad, and makes the perfect contrast. A lovely touch for maximum flavor when preparing this curry is to cut a slit in the eggplant and then to rub in a little of the spice mix. You can really taste the difference—the eggplant sucks up all the flavor of the spices while it cooks gently in the sauce.

FOR THE EGGPLANT
1 tablespoon ground coriander
1 tablespoon sesame seeds
½ teaspoon chili powder
½ tablespoon ground cumin
1½ teaspoons sea salt
¾ pound baby eggplants
1 large red onion
2 tablespoons peanut oil
1-inch piece fresh gingerroot
4 garlic cloves
3 tomatoes
a pinch of sugar

1 handful of cilantro leaves
½ lemon

FOR THE RICE
1¼ cups basmati rice

FOR THE KERALAN SPINACH AND KERNEL CORN SALAD
1 tablespoon peanut oil
1 teaspoon cumin seeds
heaped ½ cup cashews
½ pound spinach
1 red onion

1 lemon
½ red chili
heaped ⅔ cup canned whole kernel corn
1 ounce creamed coconut
sea salt

PUT THE GROUND CORIANDER, sesame seeds, chili powder, ground cumin and salt into a spice grinder, and grind to a fine powder. Remove the stalks from the baby eggplants, if you like, and cut a slit about 1 inch deep into the opposite end. Rub a little of the ground spices into the slits—use about half the spices for this. Peel and finely chop the onion.

PLACE THE OIL in a saucepan over medium heat and add the onion. Cook 4 to 5 minutes, stirring occasionally, until golden. While the onion cooks, peel the ginger and garlic, then finely chop the ginger, garlic and tomatoes. Add to the cooked onion and stir well to combine. Add the remaining ground spices, the sugar and the prepared eggplants. Stir everything together really well, then cover and simmer 20 minutes to allow the eggplants to cook through.

MEANWHILE, COOK THE RICE in boiling water 10 to 12 minutes, or until soft, or following directions on the package. Drain in a strainer and return to the pan. Cover the pan with a clean dish towel and then the lid. Let stand so the rice can fluff up.

MAKE THE SALAD while the rice cooks. Place the oil in a wok over medium heat and add the cumin seeds and cashews. Stir-fry 45 seconds, then add the spinach and a pinch of salt. Continue to stir-fry 2 to 3 minutes, or until the spinach has completely wilted. Remove from the heat and set aside.

PEEL AND FINELY CHOP THE ONION, and add it to a mixing bowl. Squeeze the juice of the lemon all over the onion, add a pinch of salt and stir well. Finely chop the chili and add it to the same bowl. Drain the kernel corn and pour it into the bowl, then add the cooked spinach, making sure you scrape all the oil and cumin into the mixing bowl. Stir well to combine, then transfer to a serving bowl. Grate the coconut evenly over the top, then cover loosely with plastic wrap and set aside.

WHEN THE EGGPLANTS HAVE COOKED, remove the lid from the pan and cook 5 minutes more, stirring occasionally, to allow the sauce to thicken. Roughly tear up the cilantro. Scatter the cooked curry with the cilantro then squeeze the juice of the lemon evenly over it. Serve with the cooked rice and the colorful salad.

NAUGHTY BUT NICE

The name says it all really. This chapter is packed with delicious desserts, fabulous drinks and killer cocktails that can all be made so fast you might as well make two at a time! Even the longest recipe only takes 30 minutes from start to finish. My Mint Tea & Lemongrass Martini takes less than 10 minutes to make and will get any party started. My Salted Caramel Chocolate Sauce (which is quite simply the greatest sauce there ever was and ever will be) poured generously over vanilla ice cream, takes only 10 minutes to make and will win you a legion of fans with every serving. My beautifully sticky Kika Cakes flavored with almonds and vanilla, and served with an Orange & Ginger Glaze, take only 25 minutes to make, proving that there is even time for a bit of gentle baking.

Vanilla Ice Cream with Salted Caramel Chocolate Sauce SERVES **4** READY IN **10 MINUTES**

This is probably the best sauce ever! A bold statement, I know, but what could be better than a wickedly sweet salted caramel sauce, loaded up with rich dark chocolate and served warm and oozing over vanilla ice cream? Find an especially good vanilla ice cream to do the sauce justice.

FOR THE ICE CREAM
17-ounce carton of awesome
  vanilla ice cream
⅓ cup hazelnuts

**FOR THE SALTED CARAMEL
  CHOCOLATE SAUCE**
⅔ cup light brown sugar
¼ cup butter
scant ¼ cup heavy cream
3½ ounces semisweet or
  bittersweet chocolate
  (85% cocoa solids)
sea salt

TAKE THE VANILLA ICE CREAM out of the freezer to soften slightly. Meanwhile, pour the sugar for the sauce into a saucepan and add 1½ tablespoons water. Bring to a boil over high heat and cook 2 to 3 minutes, shaking the pan occasionally, until all the sugar has dissolved. Roughly chop the nuts while the sugar dissolves.

REMOVE THE PAN from the heat and add the butter. Return the pan to low heat and melt the butter, beating continuously. Continue to beat another 1 minute, or until the caramel turns light brown. Add a good pinch of salt and beat well. Pour in the cream and continue to beat until velvety smooth.

BREAK UP THE CHOCOLATE into the sauce and beat continuously until it has completely melted and the sauce has thickened a little. Carefully pour the sauce into a heatproof pitcher. Divide the ice cream among four serving dishes, pour some sauce onto each portion of ice cream and scatter with the hazelnuts to serve.

Goan Explosion Truffles SERVES 4 READY IN **30 MINUTES**

Genuine truffles in 30 minutes—get in! The trick is to get your cake pan really cold and make sure that the truffle mixture goes into it in a thin layer so that it sets really fast. Scoop out the truffle mixture with a teaspoon or a fancy melon baller and drop each ball into the ground pistachios for a speedy coating. Coffee, cardamom and chili funk up these truffles. Use the maddest, greenest pistachios you can find to get the perfect Goan experience.

1 handful of ice cubes
scant ½ cup heavy cream
1 tablespoon butter

3½ ounces semisweet or
   bittersweet chocolate
   (70% cocoa solids)
¼ teaspoon espresso powder

¼ teaspoon ground cardamom
a pinch of chili powder
heaped ⅓ cup shelled green
   pistachios

PUT THE ICE in a 10-inch cake pan with a fixed base and put it into the freezer. Pour the cream into a small saucepan and add the butter. Heat the cream over medium heat 2 to 3 minutes, stirring occasionally, until the butter melts.

MEANWHILE, BREAK UP THE CHOCOLATE into a heatproof bowl. Put it into the microwave and heat a few seconds on high, or until the chocolate just starts to melt. (Alternatively, melt the chocolate in a heatproof bowl over a pan of gently simmering water, making sure the bottom of the bowl doesn't touch the water.) Remove the bowl from the microwave or steamer and add the espresso powder, cardamom and chili powder. Pour over the hot cream and beat together until thick and smooth.

WORKING AS FAST AS YOU CAN, take the cake pan out of the freezer, discard the ice and wipe the pan dry with paper towels. Pour the chocolate mixture into the pan. Spread it evenly into a thin layer no deeper than ¼ inch, otherwise it won't set in time. Put the cake pan back into the freezer 20 minutes, or until the mixture has set.

ADD THE NUTS to a food processor and blend until just coarse. Pour them into a mixing bowl. Using a teaspoon or melon baller, scoop out the truffle mixture and drop each truffle ball into the bowl of crushed nuts. Give the bowl a shake to make sure all the truffles are coated, then place on a decorative plate to serve.

Pineapple & Lime Pie SERVES **4** READY IN **20 MINUTES**

I am in love with the USA, and this dessert was inspired by the classic, key lime pie. I have used pineapple, with a hint of chili, instead of the traditional key limes, plus a no-bake crust to make it super-quick.

7½ tablespoons butter
½ pineapple
2¼ tablespoons demerara sugar
a pinch of crushed chili flakes
5 ounces graham crackers

1¾ cups heavy cream
2 tablespoons powdered sugar
½ lime

PUT 5½ TABLESPOONS of the butter in a small saucepan over medium heat and the remaining 2 tablespoons in a small skillet over medium heat.

WHILE THE BUTTER MELTS, cut the top and bottom off the pineapple, then stand it upright on your cutting board. Slice off the skin, cutting downward from top to bottom. Carefully cut out any pieces of skin left on the fruit. Cut the pineapple half in half lengthwise, then slice off the woody core so you are left with the soft fruit. Cut the pineapple flesh into small pieces and add them to the small skillet. Add the demerara sugar and a pinch of chili flakes. Stir well and cook 8 to 10 minutes, shaking the pan occasionally, until the pineapple starts to soften and the sauce has thickened. Remove from the heat and set aside to cool a little.

PUT THE GRAHAM CRACKERS into a food processor and blend to coarse crumbs while the pineapple cooks. Add to a mixing bowl, pour in the melted butter from the small saucepan and stir to combine. Line the base and sides of a 7½-inch springform cake pan with parchment paper and press the crust firmly and evenly into the bottom using the back of a spoon. Put the cake pan into the fridge while you beat the cream.

POUR THE CREAM into a large mixing bowl and add the powdered sugar. Add the zest of the lime, squeeze in the juice, then beat into firm peaks. Remove the cake pan from the fridge and fill with the cream mixture. Arrange the pineapple pieces on top, drizzle with the sauce from the pineapple, then open the side of the cake pan, remove the paper and serve.

Mango & Vanilla Coconut Pots SERVES **4**   READY IN **10 MINUTES**

Coconut and mango are best friends and appear in various guises in south-eastern Asian desserts. These fresh little pots are inspired by the many varieties I have eaten over the years. I have made my version to be as quick as possible without cutting back on any flavor. The mango is squished together with sugar and orange to soften it and intensify the taste. The sweet fruit is then topped with luscious cream that has been whipped with coconut cream to add that authentic Asian twist.

2 ripe mangoes
¼ cup powdered sugar
½ orange
generous 1¼ cups heavy cream

generous ¼ cup coconut cream
1 teaspoon vanilla extract

PEEL THE MANGO, then slice off the flesh from the sides and around the seed. Chop the flesh into bite-size pieces, then put them into a mixing bowl.

ADD HALF THE POWDERED SUGAR and squeeze in the juice of the orange. Mix together using your hands to slightly break up the mango, then set aside.

POUR THE HEAVY CREAM into a mixing bowl and beat into firm peaks. Add the coconut cream, remaining powdered sugar and the vanilla extract, and beat together. Divide the mango mixture among four glass serving dishes and add a thick layer of whipped cream to the top of each one to serve.

Pumpkin, Chocolate & Walnut Puddings SERVES **4** READY IN **25 MINUTES**

This is my version of a classic Turkish dessert of slow-braised pumpkin served with walnuts. My twist is to add chunks of bittersweet chocolate, which melt into the sweet pumpkin, topped with lovely soft whipped cream.

1 pumpkin (about 1 pound 10 ounces in weight)
½ cup heavy cream
1½ tablespoons butter
¼ cup demerara sugar

6 cloves
1 ounce semisweet or bittersweet chocolate (70% cocoa solids)
scant ½ cup walnuts

PEEL AND SEED THE PUMPKIN and cut it into 1-inch pieces. Place them in a microwaveproof bowl and add a scant ½ cup water. Cover with plastic wrap and microwave on high 10 minutes, or until the pieces are soft but haven't turned to mush. To check, poke them with a sharp knife—it should slide out very easily.

BEAT THE CREAM to soft peaks while the pumpkin cooks, and set aside. Put the butter, sugar and cloves in a skillet and place over low heat. Once the sugar starts to look a bit dry, shake the pan and it will suddenly dissolve into a liquid. Once completely dissolved, remove from the heat—it will look as though it has split from the butter, but don't worry, I promise this is how it's meant to look.

CUT TWO-THIRDS OF THE CHOCOLATE into tiny pieces and divide into 4 portions. Break up the walnuts into small pieces over a bowl using your fingers.

USING A SLOTTED SPOON, carefully transfer the cooked pumpkin to the skillet with the sugar mixture. Cook over low heat 5 minutes, stirring occasionally.

ADD ALL BUT 1 TABLESPOON of the crushed walnuts to the pumpkin and stir to combine. Divide the pumpkin mixture among four heatproof glass dessert dishes, picking out and discarding the cloves. Sprinkle a pile of chocolate all over each one and spoon one-quarter of the cream on top of each. Scatter each portion with the remaining walnuts and grate the last of the chocolate on top. Serve immediately, while the chocolate is oozing through the dessert.

Luang Prabang
Coconut Rice Pudding SERVES **4**   READY IN **20 MINUTES**

This is my express version of the classic Lao pudding. Instead of using Lao red rice and steaming it for ages, I use jasmine rice, which I parboil. Then it's finished off in coconut milk, sugar and cardamom. A good grating of nutmeg, plus some sesame seeds, fresh mango and mint leaves provide a contrast of different flavors, colors and textures to the creamy rice.

heaped ½ cup jasmine rice
scant 1 cup coconut milk
3 tablespoons superfine sugar
¼ fresh nutmeg
3 cardamom pods

2 tablespoons sesame seeds
1 large mango
1 handful of mint leaves

COOK THE RICE in boiling water 8 minutes. Meanwhile, pour the coconut milk into a saucepan. Add the sugar and grate in the nutmeg. Crush the cardamom pods by pressing down on them with the flat side of a knife blade, then add them to the coconut milk. Stir well and bring to a boil over medium heat. Reduce the heat to low and simmer gently while the rice is cooking. Drain the rice in a strainer and set aside.

MEANWHILE, PUT THE SESAME SEEDS in a skillet and toast over medium heat, shaking the pan continuously 2 to 3 minutes, or until golden. Remove from the heat and set aside.

POUR THE COOKED RICE into the coconut milk and stir well. Cover and cook gently 5 minutes. Remove the lid and cook another minute, stirring continuously, to thicken. The rice should have the consistency of a lovely oozy risotto. Remove the cardamom and discard it if you prefer.

PEEL THE MANGO while the rice finishes cooking. Slice the flesh from the sides and around the seed, and chop it into bite-size pieces. Divide the rice among four serving bowls and place a few pieces of mango on top of each serving. Scatter with the sesame seeds and mint leaves to serve.

Kika Cakes with Orange & Ginger Glaze MAKES **10 CUPCAKES** READY IN **25 MINUTES**

Express cooking can even apply to baking. Vanilla, orange and almonds make the base of my cupcakes, which soak up the yummy marmalade and ginger glaze. I prefer to use a slightly sweet marmalade to make my glaze, so the cakes take on that flavor as well.

1 egg
heaped ⅔ cup superfine sugar, plus
   1 tablespoon for the glaze
1 orange

2 teaspoons vanilla extract
1¼ cups ground almonds
1 cup all-purpose flour
¾ teaspoon baking powder

scant ½ cup marmalade
¼ teaspoon ground ginger

PREHEAT THE OVEN to 400°F. Crack the egg into a large mixing bowl and add the heaped ⅔ cup superfine sugar. Beat the egg and sugar together until fluffy and light. Add the zest of the whole orange to the bowl then squeeze in the juice of half the orange. Reserve the other half. Add the vanilla extract and ground almonds, then sift in the flour and baking powder. Gently combine to make a thick batter.

LINE A MUFFIN PAN with 10 paper baking cups. Divide the batter evenly among the cups—each cup will hold about 3 tablespoons of batter. Bake 12 to 14 minutes, or until golden on the top and cooked in the center. (They are cooked in the center when a skewer inserted into a cupcake comes out clean.)

WHILE THE CUPCAKES BAKE, put the marmalade, ground ginger and the remaining 1 tablespoon sugar into a small nonstick saucepan. Squeeze the juice of the reserved orange half into the pan and bring to a boil over medium-low heat, stirring occasionally, until the glaze ingredients dissolve together.

REMOVE THE CUPCAKES from the oven and top each one with the hot glaze. Set aside to cool a couple of minutes, then serve while still warm.

Cinnamon Fig Tarts SERVES **4** READY IN **25 MINUTES**

Figs are a staple ingredient of desserts across the Middle East, adding color, flavor and texture, and they work beautifully with spices. I have often seen the humble fig transformed into something spectacular in a dish, and it's perfect for a quick dessert. Baking figs intensifies their flavor, so I've arranged them on puff pastry that was sprinkled with demerara sugar, cinnamon and ground ginger. When cooked, they become wrapped in a wonderful, sweet, warm blanket. The clementine and mint cream heightens the flavors and accentuates the warmth of the spices.

flour, for dusting
5½ ounces puff pastry, defrosted
   if frozen
1 teaspoon demerara sugar

½ teaspoon ground cinnamon
¼ teaspoon ground ginger
6 small or 3 medium figs
1 cup heavy cream

2 clementines
2 tablespoons powdered sugar
1 small handful of mint leaves

PREHEAT THE OVEN to 400°F. Line a baking sheet with parchment paper. Crumple it up in your hands and then smooth it out onto the baking sheet again to prevent it from rolling up at the edges.

DUST THE WORK SURFACE with flour and roll out the pastry to just under ¼ inch in thickness. Cut the pastry into 4 rectangles, each measuring 4 × 6 inches, and place them on the parchment paper. Prick each pastry a few times with a fork.

ADD THE DEMERARA SUGAR, cinnamon and ginger to a bowl, stir to combine, then scatter the mixture evenly over each pastry. Cut the small figs in half, or the medium figs into quarters, and arrange 3 pieces of fig down the center of each rectangle. Bake the tarts 18 to 20 minutes, or until puffed up and golden.

MEANWHILE, POUR THE CREAM into a large mixing bowl. Add the zest of one of the clementines and squeeze in the juice of both. Sift in the powdered sugar, then whip the cream until it forms soft peaks. Save a few mint leaves for decoration and finely chop the remainder. Fold the chopped mint leaves into the whipped cream. Serve the hot tarts with a large dollop of the cream and a scattering of mint leaves.

Strawberry Layer Cakes SERVES **4**   READY IN **25 MINUTES**

These awesome crispy, creamy strawberry layer cakes are a nod to my time in Morocco. Cinnamon, orange and vanilla add the exotic flavors and turn this dessert into something out of the ordinary.

2⅓ cups strawberries
½ teaspoon ground cinnamon, plus
  a little extra for dusting
3 tablespoons powdered sugar
½ orange

2 large sheets of filo pastry,
  defrosted if frozen
scant 1¼ cups full-fat Greek yogurt
1 teaspoon vanilla extract
scant ½ cup walnut pieces

SLICE AND HULL THE STRAWBERRIES and put them into a shallow dish. Sprinkle with the cinnamon and 1 tablespoon of the powdered sugar. Squeeze in the juice of the orange and stir gently to combine. Cover with plastic wrap and set aside.

CUT THE FILO PASTRY into 12 rectangles, each measuring 3¼ × 4½ inches, then cover the filo with a damp dish towel to stop it from drying out. Heat a large skillet over medium-high heat and pan-fry the filo pastry in batches until golden and crispy. This will take about 1 to 1½ minutes on one side and 30 seconds to 1 minute on the other. Remove from the pan and set carefully aside.

PUT THE YOGURT into a mixing bowl while cooking the filo, and add the remaining powdered sugar and the vanilla. Beat together well and set aside.

WHEN ALL THE FILO IS DONE you can construct the cakes. Put a piece of cooked filo onto a serving plate and place a spoonful of yogurt on top. Spread it out evenly and cover with a thin layer of strawberries. Place another piece of filo onto the layer of strawberries, and then repeat with more yogurt and a layer of strawberries. Put a third piece of filo onto the strawberries and spread a layer of yogurt evenly on the top. Break up some of the walnuts and scatter them all over the top layer of yogurt, then sprinkle with a pinch of cinnamon. Repeat the process for the other 3 layer cakes. Serve with any remaining strawberries on the side.

TINY TOWNS, CANTO POP & SHENYANG BANANAS

Shenyang is a town in northeastern China, nestled near the borders of Mongolia and North Korea. It gets very cold, the people are unusually tall and the food is out of this world. By Chinese standards it's considered a small town—by mine it was massive. The "tiny town" of Shenyang consisted of around 8 million people, a plethora of Italian designer stores, underground shopping malls and incredible food everywhere.

It wasn't just very cold in Shenyang when I went—it was absolutely freezing! To be exact, 10 degrees below freezing during the daytime, without windchill. Being that cold meant that having a wander was a very hard thing to do. When I did stroll around it was fairly bleak, until I was ushered through what looked like a subway entrance. Bam! There it was—the main street. It was underground, so you could walk around without freezing to death. This was no ordinary shopping street, though. The retailers selling the big brands were at street level, but here underground it was neon lit, pulsating to the sound of canto pop and Chinese techno, and filled with über-cool kids decked out in Hello Kitty and glasses without any lenses.

There was street food everywhere—day-glo hot dogs and kebabs, duck heads and tongues, pancakes and rice buns, mashed potatoes and soups, noodles and salads, fruit and amazing battered bananas, which were skewered on a stick and covered in syrup and crunchy sesame seeds. They were delicious and the perfect sugar hit for such cold weather.

Shenyang Bananas with Honey & Sesame Seeds SERVES **4**   READY IN **15 MINUTES**

I have created a really quick version of the tasty snack from that under-ground shopping street in Shenyang. Sesame seeds and flour form the base of a batter to coat the bananas, and it's flavored with warming ground cloves and chili powder. The flavor of the spices lingers when the bananas are cooked, and it's somehow exaggerated by the honey drizzled over it before serving. This is express cooking at its best.

sunflower oil, for shallow-frying
1¼ cups all-purpose flour
2 tablespoons powdered sugar
¾ teaspoon ground cloves
¾ teaspoon chili powder

heaped ⅓ cup sesame seeds
1 egg
2 bananas
3 tablespoons honey

POUR THE OIL into a saucepan to a depth of ⅝ inch and place over medium-high heat. Meanwhile, sift the flour, powdered sugar, cloves and chili powder into a large mixing bowl, and add 3 tablespoons of the sesame seeds. Crack in the egg, then slowly beat in a scant 1 cup cold water to form a smooth batter.

PEEL THE BANANAS and cut them into ½-inch pieces. Put the pieces into the batter and carefully transfer them to the hot oil using a pair of long-handled tongs. Fry the bananas 30 to 45 seconds on each side, or until beautifully golden and crisp.

REMOVE THE BANANAS from the pan and put them on a dish lined with paper towels to drain. Transfer the bananas to a serving plate and drizzle with the honey. Scatter with the remaining sesame seeds to serve.

Mint Tea & Lemongrass Martini SERVES 4 READY IN 10 MINUTES

Martinis are cool. Fact. We have all seen *Mad Men*! A classic martini still eludes me, though. It's a bit like drinking rocket fuel, so I always go for a flavored one. For my express martini, I take advantage of the clean taste of vodka and add some ingredients with lovely flavors—green tea, lemongrass and mint. Adding honey and lemongrass to the green tea while it brews means that all the flavors infuse in just a couple of minutes. What you get is an instant, flavored sugar syrup—and that means a very quick martini.

2 lemongrass stalks
1 green tea bag
3 tablespoons honey
2 handfuls of ice

1 handful of mint leaves, plus a few
    extra leaves to serve
scant 1 cup vodka
1 lime

BASH EACH LEMONGRASS STALK to break it up, and roughly chop it into 1-inch pieces. Add the lemongrass to a pitcher or cocktail shaker and add the tea bag, honey and scant 1 cup boiling water. Stir well and let infuse 3 minutes.

MEANWHILE, PUT A FEW ICE CUBES into four martini glasses and let chill. Remove the tea bag from the syrup and add the mint. Pour in the vodka and squeeze in the juice of the lime. Add a large handful of ice and mix together really well.

POUR THE ICE OUT of the martini glasses and discard. Strain the mint tea and lemongrass martini evenly among the four glasses and add a few mint leaves to each glass to serve.

Burnt Lemon
& Vanilla Tequila Shots SERVES **4** READY IN **10 MINUTES**

I love tequila—a real tequila that is golden and made from 100 percent agave. This means the drink is smooth and well rounded, not like horrible paint stripper in a bottle, with a funny Mexican-hat lid and perhaps a rank insect festering at the bottom. When you work with great tequila it's important not to mess around with it too much. The vanilla in my shots accentuates the flavor of the tequila, and the burnt lemon adds to the already smoky taste of the drink. It needs balance and therefore sweetness. In an ideal world, use an agave syrup. But, failing that, a really great honey will work just as well.

2 lemons
olive oil for brushing
scant 1 cup 100% agave
  light tequila

2 tablespoons agave syrup or
  honey
1 teaspoon vanilla extract
2 handfuls of ice

CUT THE LEMONS in half and brush the flesh with a little oil. Put the lemons, cut-side down, into a nonstick skillet. Place over medium heat and cook 4 to 4½ minutes, or until the lemons are turning from a golden color to just charred. Remove the pan from the heat and set aside.

POUR THE TEQUILA into a small pitcher or cocktail shaker and add the agave syrup and vanilla extract. Carefully squeeze in the juice of the lemons and run a teaspoon around the flesh side to get all the sticky pieces out. Add the ice and mix well. Pour into four tall shot glasses and serve immediately—*Salud*!

Hot & Spicy Bourbon SERVES **4** READY IN **5 MINUTES**

Bourbon has been my drink of the month for quite some time now. It has a good smoky flavor that comes from the charred oak barrels it is aged in. The hot, sticky Kentucky air speeds up this aging process, so the bourbon ends up being a relatively young drink. This gives it a beautifully smooth and mellow taste. As you can tell, I am seriously into it! In this delicious hot drink the star anise, cinnamon and cloves accentuate the taste of the bourbon, and the orange and honey provide the classic accompanying flavors. This is advanced hot-toddy drinking, people!

4 star anise
4 cinnamon sticks
8 cloves
1 orange

1 cup bourbon
4 tablespoons honey

BOIL SOME WATER. Meanwhile, divide the star anise, cinnamon sticks and cloves among four mugs.

USING A PEELER, peel 4 strips of orange zest, give them a twist and add them to the mugs. Cut 4 thin slices from the orange and put one slice in each mug.

DIVIDE THE BOURBON and honey between the mugs, then fill each mug to the top with boiling water. Give each mug of hot and spicy bourbon a good stir with its cinnamon stick and serve.

INDEX

Acknowledgments

THANK YOU TO: Annie and Mike; Lizzie and Amish; Little South Island BBQ for the inspiration and good times; Heather at Villa Dinari; my godson Max; Duncan Baird Publishers for doing it again; Rita and family in Goa; Gail in Fez; my brother Tom and his gorgeous wife Rach, for always putting me up.

Picture Credits

KEY: **T** = Top **B** = Bottom **L** = Left **R** = Right

All location photography by John Gregory-Smith except for the following:

Page 34 holy cow (Kelvintt/Dreamstime.com); **p. 35** cow in road (Paop/Dreamstime.com); **p. 45 L** Grand Bazaar stall (Wojtek Chmielewski/Shutterstock), **BR** man with food cart (Jim Snyders/Alamy); **p. 119 TR** Jamaa el-Fnaa square (Alex Andrei/Shutterstock), **BR** baskets of spices (Heatherfaye/iStockphoto), **L** baskets and mounds of spices (nolimitspictures/iStockphoto); **p. 151 TR** chilies (Stevenallan/iStockphoto), **R** Mexican man (Frans Lemmens/Corbis), **B** market (Christian Kober/Robert Harding World Imagery/Corbis).